Switzerland

Switzerland

BY LURA ROGERS SEAVEY

Enchantment of the World™
Second Series

CHILDREN'S PRESS®

An Imprint of Scholastic Inc.

Frontispiece: **Mountain lake, Uri canton**

Consultant: Jonathan Steinberg, PhD, Walter H. Annenberg Professor of Modern European History, Emeritus, University of Pennsylvania, Philadelphia, Pennsylvania
Please note: All statistics are as up-to-date as possible at the time of publication.

Book production by The Design Lab

Library of Congress Cataloging-in-Publication Data
Names: Rogers Seavey, Lura, author.
Title: Switzerland / by Lura Rogers Seavey.
Description: New York, NY : Children's Press, a division of Scholastic
  [2017] | Series: Enchantment of the world | Includes bibliographical
  references and index.
Identifiers: LCCN 2016000985 | ISBN 9780531218877 (library binding)
Subjects: LCSH: Switzerland—Juvenile literature.
Classification: LCC DQ17 .S43 2017 | DDC 949.4—dc23
LC record available at http://lccn.loc.gov/2016000985

1 2 3 4 5 6 7 8 9 10 R 26 25 24 23 22 21 20 19 18 17

Astronomical clock, Bern

Contents

Left to right: **Hikers, Rhine River, farmer, Alps, alpenhorns**

CHAPTER 1

The Swiss Way

A TRAIN SPEEDS THROUGH A TUNNEL BENEATH towering snowcapped peaks. Bankers sit around a conference table discussing billion-dollar deals. Young people relax at a café on a narrow cobblestone street. Switzerland is all this, and much more.

Sitting in the mountains of central Europe, Switzerland has a unique history and place in the world today. Switzerland has long had a policy of neutrality, taking no sides and protecting itself while larger, more powerful countries fought and argued around it. In part because of this neutrality, many international organizations are based in Switzerland.

Switzerland itself is made up of twenty-six cantons. These are like U.S. states, except they are much more independent of national control. Each has its own laws, and its own culture. Switzerland is divided in other ways as well; it has four official languages: German, French, Italian, and Rumantsch. Although most Swiss speak at least two languages, communication can sometimes be difficult.

Opposite: **A train crosses a bridge over a deep ravine in the Alps. Trains and cars use many tunnels and bridges to travel from Switzerland to Italy.**

At Ballenberg, in west-central Switzerland, there are no trillion-dollar banks or great feats of engineering. There are no presidents gathering to make history, or Olympic medals to be won. But there is hard work and ingenuity. There is meticulous craftsmanship. There is diversity and cooperation. These qualities are at the heart of everything that is Swiss, and have been for a very long time.

Ballenberg is home to a unique museum—a living history village that brings Switzerland's rich past to life. And although it may seem like the opposite of today's Switzerland, Ballenberg actually shows how the values of yesterday have shaped the nation of today.

Visitors step into a village set at the feet of the Alps and find traditional houses, farms, and workshops that represent each of the country's regions. These buildings show the architectural diversity through various times in history and in different regions. They also show what people did in the past.

Inside one house, workers are busy turning the silk of silkworms into thread, making flax into linen, and weaving these threads into fabric, while others sew the fabrics into clothes. In another, people turn fresh milk from the cows grazing nearby into butter and cheese, while bakers transform freshly harvested grain into loaves of bread. At the center of the village, a pharmacist sits in his apothecary explaining the science of herbal medicine. Next door, a potter forms bowls on his wheel, while artists paint scenes of farm life on chairs and stools that were trees yesterday.

Outdoors, the farm is worked by hand with simple tools and animal power. Men are chopping wood and separating out the pieces that are perfect for the woodcarvers and shingle makers. In the barn just out back, a woman is shearing a sheep so she can make a wool blanket. Her friend is in the chestnut grove next door, tucking a few of the nuts from the harvest away in her apron to be roasted later on the fire.

Visitors at Ballenberg watch as the wool is sheared off a sheep.

Like any country, Switzerland's past had its good times and its troubles, and Ballenberg reminds visitors that although the simple life of yesterday had some appeal, progress is a good thing, too. An exhibit about the *Verdingkinder*, or "contract children," recalls the time not so long ago when children were taken from their homes and forced into a life of hard labor on farms far from their families. Until the 1970s, children of poor families, especially of single mothers, were taken by the state and placed in this "foster care" system, and parents could do nothing to stop it.

Ballenberg doesn't varnish Switzerland's long history into an ideal theme-park world. Instead, it reminds the families, tourists, and schoolchildren who visit today that the good life they have in modern Switzerland comes from a long heritage of hard work and cooperation. And that the basic values that molded the country are just as important today as they were a hundred years ago.

CHAPTER 2

Up, Down, and All Around

SWITZERLAND IS A SMALL COUNTRY THAT LIES IN the middle of Europe. It is bordered by Germany to the north, France to the west, Italy to the south, and Austria and Liechtenstein to the east. The country covers a total area of 15,940 square miles (41,285 square kilometers), which is a little more than the size of the U.S. states of New Hampshire and Connecticut combined.

Seventy percent of the area of Switzerland is mountain. It is so mountainous that the American author Mark Twain once joked, "Switzerland would be a mighty big place if it were ironed flat."

The Jura mountain range extends along part of the border with France. The Swiss section of the Alps runs along the entire border with Italy and the borders with France, Liechtenstein, and Austria. The only part of the country that is not mountainous is the Swiss Plateau, also known as the Mittelland. Occupying north-central Switzerland, it is where most of the population lives.

Opposite: **Rich green valleys separate the rocky mountain peaks in Switzerland.**

Switzerland's Geographic Features

Area: 15,940 square miles (41,285 sq km)

Greatest Distance East–West: 213 miles (343 km)

Greatest Distance North–South: 138 miles (222 km)

Lowest Elevation: Lake Maggiore, 640 feet (195 m) above sea level

Highest Elevation: Dufourspitze, 15,203 feet (4,634 m) above sea level

Longest Lake: Lake Geneva, 45 miles (73 km)

Longest River: Rhine, 233 miles (375 km) within Switzerland

Largest Glacier: Aletsch Glacier, 66 square miles (171 sq km)

Average Daily High Temperature: In Zürich, 38°F (3°C) in January, 75°F (24°C) in July

Average Daily Low Temperature: In Zürich, 28°F (–2°C) in January, 57°F (14°C) in July

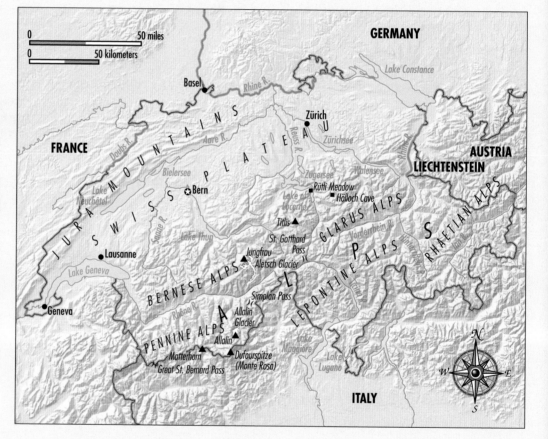

White-Tipped Majesty

When many people think of Switzerland, they think of the Alps, the largest mountain chain in Europe. The Alps cover 60 percent of Switzerland. The mountains' snowcapped peaks are the source of their name, since the word *alp* comes from the Latin word for "white." Within Switzerland, the Alps have forty-eight peaks that top 13,000 feet (4,000 meters). The tallest is Dufourspitze, which soars to 15,203 feet (4,634 m) above sea level.

The Alps are more than just statistics. They have influenced Swiss culture by separating the country from its neighbors, and they have influenced Swiss history by deterring invaders. They have become a symbol of the country and a tourist destination that brings visitors year-round.

Two mountaineers make their way along a ridge in the Swiss Alps. The entire Alps chain passes through eleven European countries.

Top Peaks

Jungfrau 13,641 feet (4,158 m)

Jungfrau (below) is the site of Europe's highest railroad station, which sits at an elevation of 11,722 feet (3,573 m) above sea level in Jungfraujoch, a small village near the mountain's summit. The village also holds Europe's highest post office with its own postal code as well as hotels, restaurants, and weather research stations. Visitors can walk through tunnels to reach ski areas and the Ice Palace in the Aletsch Glacier.

Matterhorn: 14,692 feet (4,478 m)

The Matterhorn's (right) towering crooked peak is a symbol of the Swiss Alps. The viewing station atop the mountain is the highest in Europe. The Matterhorn's glacial grotto, or cave, features ice sculptures, and the peak features year-round skiing.

Allalin: 11,341 feet (3,457 m)

Mount Allalin is home to the world's largest ice grotto, a cave covered with ice. The mountain also has the world's highest revolving restaurant and year-round skiing. Allalin Glacier lies on the mountain. In 1965, a massive avalanche raced down this glacier, killing eighty-eight people in the area below.

Titlis: 10,046 feet (3,062 m)

Visitors can take a gondola to reach the top of Titlis. This is the only gondola in Switzerland that revolves as it rises. Titlis features beautiful glacial caves, where visitors can walk through eerie blue tunnels, going deep into the ice. Titlis also has Europe's highest suspension bridge, the Cliff Walk, which is located at about 10,000 feet (3,000 m) above sea level.

Over the Alps

Ancient peoples found ways to get across the Alps. They wore trails across the lowest points between the towering peaks. Over the centuries, as these foot trails were used by traders, travelers, and invading armies, the most heavily traveled ones widened into roads for wagons and carriages. These passes made Switzerland prosperous, as the Swiss controlled some of the most important trade routes between the Mediterranean countries to the south and the rest of Europe.

The most accessible of these passes are still impor-tant travel routes, with tunnels boring through mountains enabling cars, trucks, and trains to travel easily. Some of these

A road snakes through St. Gotthard Pass, which cuts through the mountains, connecting the German-speaking and Italian-speaking regions of Switzerland.

An avalanche rumbles down a mountainside in Switzerland. An average of twenty-two people die in avalanches in Switzerland each year.

tunnels connect Switzerland with Italy and France, while others connect different valleys within Switzerland. In all, 109 roads pass over the Swiss Alps. Eighteen of them are at elevations higher than 6,500 feet (2,000 m).

Some of these high-altitude passes are closed in the winter, when deep snow and high winds make it impossible to keep them plowed. Swiss engineers have been very resourceful in finding ways to keep the most important routes open. In places where avalanches or snow slides are common, roads are protected by strong, reinforced roofs. Tunnels bypass some of the most exposed summits.

Major international rail routes include the Simplon, the St. Gotthard, and the Great St. Bernard passes. One of the most ambitious tunnels shortened the route across the steep St. Gotthard Pass. Engineers built an ingenious tunnel that carried trains to the top of the pass in a looping pattern, as if

All Aboard!

One railway tunnel through the Alps of southern Switzerland carries cars on a "piggyback" train. Drivers arrive in the town of Kandersteg and drive their cars right onto an open train car. They drive off again in Goppenstein at the other end of the Lötschberg Tunnel.

they were ascending a spiral staircase. Passengers could look out and see the town of Wassen from three different levels as the train came out of the tunnel briefly at each loop. In 2016, an even more daring feat of engineering opened, short-

The first tunnel at St. Gotthard Pass was built in 1880. It stretched 9 miles (15 km) through the rock.

The Birth of Mountains

The outside layer of the earth is broken up into large chunks called tectonic plates. These plates are constantly in motion in relation to one another, and as they move, they change the shape of the land.

The Jura Mountains and the Alps were formed by the intense pressure of tectonic plates pushing together, forcing the land upward. Later, large sheets of ice called glaciers crept across the landscape, carving deep U-shaped valleys in the landscape. Rivers flowing off the melting glaciers slowly eroded the soil, creating V-shaped valleys. In some places in Switzerland, rain washed away softer minerals, leaving harder rock standing alone in strange formations that look like rough towers.

ening the train route dramatically by tunneling through the base of the mountains instead of climbing over the pass. This allows freight trains to carry twice as much weight as before. Stretching 35 miles (56 km), it is the world's longest tunnel.

Between the Mountains

Between the many mountain chains in Switzerland is the Swiss Plateau region. It is also called the Mittelland, which translates from German literally as "middle-land." The Swiss Plateau sits in the north-central part of the country. Many plateaus are flat, but the Swiss Plateau is actually quite hilly and varied. Although the Swiss Plateau makes up roughly one-third of the nation's land area, around two-thirds of the population lives there. Half of the plateau region is used for agriculture, about a quarter is forest, and less than one-fifth is used for homes and businesses.

Ice Giants

Glaciers are ancient masses of solid ice that exist in some of the world's coldest places. Switzerland has over 1,000 square miles (2,600 sq km) of glaciers. The largest are in the southern part of the country, including Aletsch Glacier, which covers 66 square miles (171 sq km). Although glaciers appear to be as permanent as the mountains, they are in fact huge rivers of ice, always on the move. Many of Switzerland's valleys were carved by glaciers.

Crops such as rye grow on the rolling hills of the Swiss Plateau.

Switzerland's Largest Cities

The largest city in Switzerland is Zürich (below), which has a population of 391,400. About one-third of the people in the city are "permanent foreign residents," not Swiss citizens. This population is made up of 166 nationalities and many languages are spoken, but the official language is German. Zürich has been named one of the three most expensive cities in the world, but it is also one of the most livable, with a lot of green space, an active art scene, and many lively restaurants and cafés. Zürich is a center of banking and education.

Geneva is the nation's second-largest city with a population of 194,600. This city houses the headquarters of dozens of international organizations, including the Red Cross and United Nations. As a result, the city is known for its cultural diversity and is home to people of 184 different nationalities. All together, nearly half the people in Geneva are foreign nationals. The city has a rich history, with Celtic people living there more than two thousand years ago. It became the birthplace of the Swiss watchmaking industry and today is a world finan-

cial and scientific center. French is the official language in Geneva. The second most spoken language is English.

Basel (above), Switzerland's third-largest city, home to approximately 168,600 people, sits on the Rhine River in the northwest, on the border with Germany and France. Like other Swiss cities, it has a large foreign population—about 35 percent. German is the city's primary language. One of Switzerland's oldest cities, Basel has beautiful medieval architecture, including the Gate of Spalen, an ancient part of the city walls, and a cathedral that was first built in the 1000s and rebuilt after an earthquake in 1356. The city is the site of several esteemed universities, including the University of Basel, the nation's oldest university. It is also the center of the nation's chemical and medicine industries.

Another French-speaking city, Lausanne, has a population of 133,900. About 42 percent of these people are permanent foreign residents. The city, in western Switzerland, sits overlooking Lake Geneva, and is the home of the International Olympic Committee and the Olympic Museum. Because of this, it is also the headquarters of many Swiss sports organizations. The city has many fine historic buildings, including a cathedral that was built in the 1200s.

Unlike snowpack that melts in the spring, the glaciers remain year-round. But in recent decades, the earth's average temperature has been rising, and as it rises, the glaciers are melting. The melting of glaciers around the world means rising sea levels and changing ecosystems. In Switzerland, the melting of these giants means the loss of some of the world's most beautiful natural sites, like the blue caverns at Titlis.

At Titlis, visitors can descend into a glacier and walk through a long glacial cave. The cave looks blue because light bends when it passes through ice, shifting to a bluer hue.

Chillon Castle sits on the eastern end of Lake Geneva. The oldest parts of the castle were built more than a thousand years ago.

Water, Water Everywhere

Between the dripping glaciers, natural springs, and mountain precipitation, Switzerland is full of streams and rivers that flow into the plateau from the higher elevations. Many of Europe's most important rivers begin high in the mountains of Switzerland. These include the Rhine, which forms part of Switzerland's border with Austria and Liechtenstein before heading north and eventually emptying into the North Sea. The Rhône flows west before ending up in the Mediterranean Sea, while the Inn flows east, joining the Danube, central Europe's largest river. The Ticino flows south, joining the Po, the longest river in Italy.

Switzerland's rivers and streams feed hundreds of lakes, many of which are small pockets of water scattered throughout the mountains. Others are large, like Lake Geneva, which covers 224 square miles (580 sq km) and has the cities of Geneva and Lausanne on its shores. Lake Constance, the next-largest lake, lies on the border with both Austria and Germany. In all, Switzerland has more than 1,500 lakes.

Because Switzerland has so much water flowing down from the mountains, the Swiss harness this energy. Many lakes have been created by dams that were constructed to generate hydro-electric power. The dams force the river water to turn turbines, which generate electricity. So much electricity is created in these hydroelectric plants that it is exported to surrounding countries.

Dams such as the Emosson Dam in southern Switzerland were built to generate electricity. About three-fifths of the energy used in Switzerland comes from hydroelectricity.

Under the Mountains

Wherever water is moving, there is earth being washed away and reshaped. Runoff from glaciers has been working away the rock over tens of thousands of years, resulting in steep ravines and gorges. Where the rock is softer, it wears away more easily, resulting in underground caves. Switzerland has more than three thousand caves. In the late 1800s, cave explorers, who are called spelunkers, discovered many of them. About a dozen of these caves can be safely explored by visitors today. The Hölloch Cave in central Switzerland is the nation's most visited cave. A small part of its total 93 miles (150 km) is lit so visitors can see the beautiful cave formations.

Sun and Snow

Although Switzerland is a relatively small country, its mountainous geography causes temperatures and weather patterns to vary greatly from one location to the next. At the top of the tallest mountains, temperatures can reach as low as –44 degrees Fahrenheit (–42 degrees Celsius), while the valleys of the Ticino region, in the south of Switzerland, can reach 95°F (35°C) or above.

Defending Nature

Pro Natura, Switzerland's largest conservation organization, was created in 1909 to support the establishment of the Swiss National Park. Since then, the organization has worked to preserve Switzerland's environment. One way it does this is by lobbying, or putting political pressure on the government, to help ensure that strong laws are passed. Pro Natura has also worked to create more than six hundred nature reserves. In addition, the organization educates the public about environmental issues through its nature centers, publications, and school outreach programs. Today, Pro Natura has one hundred thousand members. All of the leaders are volunteers.

Zürich, in the north-central part of the country, gets an average of 45 inches (114 centimeters) of precipitation a year, mostly in the form of rain. Jungfrau Mountain, in contrast, receives 163 inches (414 cm) of precipitation a year—all snow. In general, the western part of the country tends to get more precipitation as winds carry clouds heavy with moisture in from the Atlantic Ocean. When clouds move north from the Mediterranean, they are stopped by the wall of Alps and drop their rain. This leaves the area north of the Alps dry, warm, and windy. This atmospheric phenomenon often creates a dry, warm wind known as the foehn, which blows down from the northern side of the Alps. Foehn winds can raise temperatures dramatically in just a few minutes.

A rainy day in Geneva. The city receives about 40 inches (100 cm) of rain per year, spread evenly across the months.

CHAPTER 3

The Natural World

SWITZERLAND'S CLIMATE AND LANDSCAPE VARY tremendously, providing habitat for diverse plants and animals. Different types of life are well suited to its particular temperature, soil content, and type of terrain. As a result, the types of plants and animals found change as the elevation and climate change. Glaciers that sit at lower elevations may also limit plant life by acting like a giant refrigerator, cooling the surrounding area.

Opposite: **Bistort is a wildflower that grows throughout Europe and parts of western Asia. Its long, brushlike blooms appear in late spring and summer.**

From Palm Trees to Lichens

Switzerland's southern regions, such as Ticino, enjoy an almost Mediterranean climate, with warm, dry summers and cool, wet winters. In these areas, warm-weather plants like palm trees grow. Just to the north is the alpine region, where elevation and temperature limit which plants are able to thrive. Trees become sparse above elevations of 5,900 feet (1,800 m), with mostly only brush and mountain grasses growing. Above 7,000

Symbol of the Alps

The edelweiss is the unofficial national flower of Switzerland. The alpine edelweiss's scientific name, *Leontopodium alpinum*, is Latin for "Alpine lion's tooth" because of the shape of its leaves. These leaves are actually what most people think are the flower. They are silver-white and cluster around a very tiny flower in the center. Edelweiss grows at high altitudes, generally ranging from 5,000 to 10,000 feet (1,500 to 3,000 m), and prefers south-facing slopes. It can be found on slopes throughout the Alps and has become a symbol of the mountain chain.

Edelweiss was once picked by young suitors as a sign of affection and commitment. It is said that many young men fell to their death trying to pluck a flower from an alpine ledge, which made a gift of this flower a sign of great bravery. It has also been used in folk medicine, for it is believed to help digestive problems. Modern science has found that edelweiss has several

valuable properties, such as the ability to absorb sometimes-harmful ultraviolet light at high altitudes. Its extract is used in some sunscreens and other skincare products.

feet (2,100 m), many types of wildflowers flourish, such as the edelweiss, a fuzzy white flower that grows on rocky slopes. Above 10,500 feet (3,200 m), only lichen and mosses grow.

Forested areas make up approximately 30 percent of Switzerland's land area, and have been protected by federal law for over 140 years. Alpine tree coverage is especially important in preventing avalanches, which threaten the valleys below year-round. The higher altitudes have evergreen trees that can withstand the harsh environment, while lower regions have a mixture of evergreens and deciduous trees, or those that lose their leaves.

The Mighty Chestnut

Part of southern Switzerland lies south of the Alps. This region has a different climate than other parts of the country. Beautiful chestnut forests thrive on the mountainsides at altitudes of up to 3,000 feet (900 m), warmed by the large lakes below them.

For centuries, chestnuts were an important staple food in the area. Some chestnuts were eaten fresh in the fall when they were harvested. They could be either boiled or roasted over the fire. The chestnuts were also dried for use all winter long. The dried chestnuts could be ground into nutritious flour for bread and pasta.

The chestnut harvest was a time for the whole community to work together, gathering the nuts and taking them to sheds called *grà*, where they were kept over low fires until they were dry enough to store.

Nothing was wasted from the valuable chestnut trees: Fallen leaves were used as bedding for cattle, and the wood was used for furniture and tools. Some chestnuts were exported to be sold by chestnut vendors on city streets as far away as Paris, France.

By the mid-twentieth century, chestnuts became less important as a food, and people stopped tending the chestnut forests. But recently, people in the Ticino region have rediscovered these beautiful forests. They take care of the trees, replanting them when they fall, and creating walking routes along the hillsides and through the forests. Ticino chefs are creating new dishes using chestnuts, and the old harvest festivals have been revived. In October, the entire city of Lugano celebrates chestnuts with street vendors selling them roasted and made into delicious desserts, noodles, and candies. People decorate with the prickly burrs from chestnut trees. Visitors follow the Chestnut Trail, stopping at restaurants that serve special chestnut menus during the festival.

The European pine marten has sharp claws that help it climb trees.

Animals High and Low

Switzerland's plateau region and forested land are home to fox, deer, and other small animals like the marten. The pine marten is related to the mink and badger, and eats plants as well as small rodents and other creatures. Wolves and rabbits were once common there but have been hunted so heavily that they are now rare. The beaver was hunted so extensively

Furry Heroes

Saint Bernards are working dogs that were originally bred in the Swiss Alps. They are very large dogs, and much of what they did was help push snow from the road, keeping passes clear in the winter so that travelers could get through safely. Beginning in the 1700s they were used as guides and to help locate people who had lost their way. They could find lost travelers and guide them to safety, even when snow and fog blinded their human companions.

that it was eliminated completely from Switzerland but was eventually reintroduced and can now be found around many ponds and streams at lower elevations.

The mountains are home to mammals that are particularly suited for the steep, rocky terrain and can handle the low temperatures. The alpine ibex, a type of large goat, lives at elevations of between 5,000 and 10,000 feet (1,500 to 3,000 m).

Both male and female alpine ibexes have horns, but the males' horns grow much longer. They can reach 37 inches (98 cm) in length.

Marmot Life

The alpine marmot is a relative of the squirrel. It lives in the grasslands of the Alps at elevations of between 2,000 and 10,500 feet (600 and 3,200 m). Because of the extreme cold of their habitat, these creatures have evolved to hibernate during the winter. They snuggle together to conserve body heat, but are able to survive even if their body temperature drops as low as 41°F (5°C). Their heart rate slows from their normal 180 to 200 beats per minute to around 30 to 40 beats per minute to conserve energy throughout the winter. About three-quarters of their diet is made of flowering plants that contain a lot of fat, giving them the calories they need for hibernation.

Alpine marmots are very social and live in family units with parents and many of their offspring. Their burrows consist of a series of interconnected tunnels that have specific "rooms" for different uses, such as a nursery for babies and a hibernation room. They also have scattered smaller burrows that they use as places to quickly

hide from predators, especially the golden eagle. In an alpine marmot colony, at least one member of the group is always watching the sky. To warn others of an eagle above, the marmots make a loud, high-pitched whistle.

Male ibexes are much larger than females. Ibexes are known for being able to climb the steepest of slopes.

The chamois is a smaller goatlike animal that lives on the steep rocky mountainsides. Both males and females have horns, which grow only 10 to 12 inches (25 to 30 cm) long. The chamois may also be found roaming the lower forested regions from time to time, foraging for fresh greens.

Nearly two hundred species of birds live in Switzerland. Common birds like the finch, sparrow, crow, and wren can be found in the plateau region and lower elevations. The cuckoo and lark are rarer. The golden eagle is often seen soaring high above mountain meadows, on the hunt for rodents.

Another large alpine bird, the bearded vulture, was at one time completely hunted out of Switzerland because people thought that it killed livestock and even human babies. It is now known that the vulture eats only carrion, the remains of an animal that has already died. The species was successfully reintroduced to the country in 1991. Though these large birds don't snatch live animals, their eating habits can be dramatic. They cannot break bones with their beaks, so instead they drop their meals from high in the air onto rocks below. This shatters the bones so the vulture can swallow the smaller pieces. Bone marrow, the tissue inside the bones, makes up a large part of its diet.

One of a Kind

Founded in 1914, the Swiss National Park remains the only national park in Switzerland. For more than a hundred years, it has been a sanctuary where native plants and animals can exist without the interference of humans. It is in the Alps in eastern Switzerland, covering a pristine area that is equal parts rock, forest, and meadow.

Rules for park visitors are strict, and there is a steep fine for anyone who violates them. Pets are forbidden, and hikers cannot stray from the designated paths. Visitors may not take any of the local plant life, even deadwood. Camping and fires are not allowed. Posted signs frequently remind hikers of the park motto: "Take nothing but pictures, leave nothing but footprints on marked trails."

CHAPTER 4

The Road to Unity

ONE HUNDRED FIFTY THOUSAND YEARS AGO, Neanderthals, a species of early humans, left tools, animal bones, and their skeletons in caves throughout the mountains of what is now Switzerland. The plentiful caves provided welcome shelter, while the region's many rivers and lakes provided a bounty of fresh water and fish. By about seventy thousand years ago, however, thick glaciers had spread across the land.

About 12,000 years ago, toward the end of the glacial period, modern humans arrived in the area. As the glaciers melted, human culture moved beyond hunting and gathering. By around 5000 BCE, modern humans were making more advanced tools like the wheel. They began to shift from nomadic life to more permanent settlements, raising livestock and growing crops such as corn for food.

Opposite: **Ancient people in what is now Switzerland were hunters. About fifteen thousand years ago, they carved these reindeer antlers into spearheads.**

Celts, Romans, and Franks

Over the centuries, many different groups settled in what is now Switzerland. One of the earliest groups was a Celtic tribe called the Helvetians. (The Celts were a large group of related people who arose in central Europe and spread over most of the continent.) The Helvetians first arrived in Switzerland around 100 BCE. They grouped their dwellings in the hills and built defensive walls around them. Their society was technologically advanced and well organized. The Helvetians became known for their metalwork and tools.

The Romans, who were based to the south in what is now Italy, were the most powerful group in Europe. In time, the Roman Empire spread across most of the continent. In 58 BCE, the Romans gained control of Helvetic territory, which they called Helvetia. The Romans remained powerful in the region for more than four centuries. Many of Switzerland's major cities were founded during this time. The locations of these settlements were chosen because they were along trade routes or had a strategic advantage. Avenches (then known as Aventicum) in

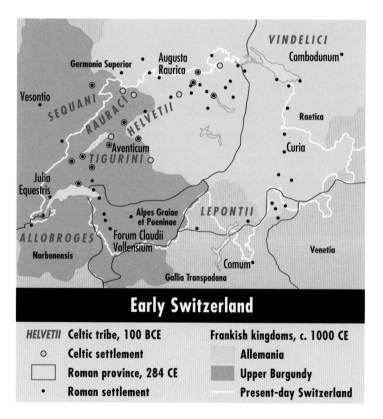

Early Switzerland

HELVETII	Celtic tribe, 100 BCE	Frankish kingdoms, c. 1000 CE	
○	Celtic settlement		Allemania
▭	Roman province, 284 CE		Upper Burgundy
•	Roman settlement		Present-day Switzerland

western Switzerland was the Roman capital of Helvetia. Ruins of a Roman amphitheater and public baths can still be seen in the town. Helvetia was relatively peaceful until around 260 CE, when Germanic tribes began to attack. By 400 CE, the Romans had lost control of most of the area.

A Germanic tribe called the Franks eventually took over the western part of the region, settling in modern-day eastern France and French-speaking Switzerland. The Alamannen tribe took over the northern section and beyond, creating Germany and today's German-speaking Switzerland.

Augusta Raurica is an ancient Roman settlement near Basel. At its height, the city was home to about twenty thousand people and included a theater, temples, baths, and workshops.

The Swiss Confederation

Nestled in between mountain chains, Switzerland was cut off from the centers of European power, so little attention was given to the area by Europe until the eleventh century. Instead, four noble families gained control of different parts

The leaders of Schwyz, Uri, and Unterwalden take the legendary Oath of Rütli. The oath is central to Swiss national identity.

of Switzerland. These families were the Zähringen, the Savoy, the Kyburg, and the Habsburgs. They founded cities and monasteries. As the cities grew and more trade routes were established through the Alps, the mountain passes became valued as connections between the Mediterranean and the rest of Europe.

By the middle of the 1200s, the Habsburg dynasty had become dominant in Switzerland. It set its sights on taking over the Uri and Schwyz Valleys in what is now central Switzerland. These areas had been enjoying relative freedom under the local rule, and they did not want to give that up.

In 1291, representatives of Uri, Schwyz, and another region called Unterwalden met and affirmed a pact to preserve their independence and allow no foreign judges in their communities. Legend calls this the Oath of Rütli, named for the meadow where they gathered. This is considered the beginning of the Swiss Confederation.

Over the next sixty years, eight more cantons joined the confederation, including Lucerne, Zürich, Glarus, Zug, and Bern. As controlling powers changed, the confederacy watched for opportunities to grow. When neighboring territories became vulnerable, the existing members of the confederation expanded. The member cantons did not always agree on who should get the opportunity to expand.

Eventually, conflicts arose among the cantons about whether they should allow new cantons join the confederation. Some rural regions felt threatened by the larger cities. No new members were allowed until 1481, when Fribourg and

A view of Zürich from about 1500. At the time, the city was home to about five thousand people.

The Legend of William Tell

Every Swiss child knows the story of brave William Tell, who defied the reeve, a representative of Habsburg authority. The story is told in comic books and television cartoons, performed at festivals and in school plays. William Tell is a folk hero, credited with moving medieval mountain villagers toward joining in a confederation that would become Switzerland.

The legend tells how in 1307 Tell was arrested when he didn't bow to the hat that was posted as a symbol of the Habsburg emperor's power over the villages. The reeve then ordered Tell to shoot an apple off his son's head. Tell did this, but was taken prisoner anyway. He escaped, shot the reeve with an arrow, and fled to gather other leaders to sign the Oath of Rütli, swearing to defy the Habsburgs' authority.

Most historians doubt that Tell really existed, let alone shot an apple from his son's head. The story was first recorded in 1569, more than 250 years later, and the Oath of Rütli was not signed by anyone named Tell. The story of the apple is a much older tale, which probably blended into the legend of William Tell as it was told and retold. But real or myth, the story of William Tell's bravery has become an inspirational symbol of Swiss determination and unity.

Solothurn joined. Some rural areas and towns were on the verge of a civil war, but a religious hermit named Nicholas of Flüe convinced the leaders to stop fighting and compromise instead. This led to the signing of the Diet of Stans, a treaty that eased tensions and avoided civil war. The cantons agreed that they would not make separate alliances, strengthening the union.

In time, Switzerland became a power in central Europe. Everyone in Switzerland owned arms, and the Swiss always seemed ready to fight. In the late 1400s, the Swiss

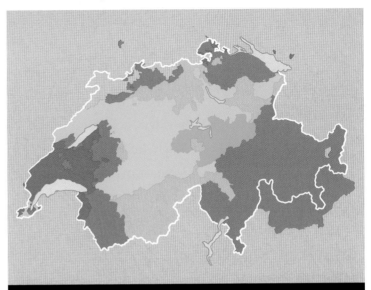

Expansion of the Swiss Confederation

- Confederation of Uri, Schwyz, and Unterwalden, 1291
- Added to Swiss Confederation, 1313–1414
- Added 1415–1450
- Added 1451–1535
- Added 1536–1570
- —— Present-day Switzerland

The Vatican's Swiss Guards

Swiss forces were highly respected and were sometimes hired by other countries as mercenaries, or paid soldiers. This practice was outlawed in 1874, with one exception: Swiss soldiers are still hired to stand guard at Vatican City, the center of the Roman Catholic Church. The Swiss Guards have been responsible for protecting the pope, the leader of the church, for more than five hundred years. This duty is a source of pride for the Swiss, even those who are not Roman Catholic.

resisted the growing power of the Habsburgs, whose power by then was centered in the Netherlands. In 1499, the Habsburg ruler Maximilian I joined the Swabian League, a group of German princes, to attack Graubünden. This was a region in the east of what is now Switzerland that was then a Swiss ally. This attack set off the Swabian War. Peace was soon declared. The regions of Basel and Schaffhausen were allowed into the Swiss Confederation because of their loyalty and military support during the Swabian War. Appenzell joined the confederation in 1513. After that, it was nearly three hundred years until any more cantons joined the confederation.

The Swiss defeated the troops of Maximilian I at the Battle of Dornach in July 1499. It was the last battle of the Swabian War.

Huldrych Zwingli preaches in Zürich. Zwingli was already criticizing the Roman Catholic Church in his sermons when he took a position in Zürich in 1518.

The Protestant Reformation

Throughout the Middle Ages, the leaders of the Roman Catholic Church in Rome were powerful throughout Europe, governing what people believed and how they lived their lives. But the church had grown corrupt as it grew powerful, and some practices seemed intended primarily to enrich the church.

By the 1500s, some people within the church were protesting the corruption. In Germany, a religious leader named Martin Luther openly challenged the church, hoping to reform some of its practices. This movement became known as the Protestant Reformation, because people were "protesting" the practices of

John Calvin advocated a strict form of Protestantism, which prohibited activities such as dancing.

the Roman Catholic Church and wanted to "reform" it.

In Switzerland, religious leaders Huldrych Zwingli and John Calvin took the ideas of the Protestant Reformation even farther. Zwingli, a priest in Zürich, sought to rid the church of corruption and change its practice. Zwingli believed Christianity should focus on Bible teachings. He argued that people should read the Bible themselves to understand its teachings, not just hear about it in sermons. Zwingli also simplified the mass in his church. John Calvin was a French lawyer and religious scholar who moved to Switzerland in 1533. From his eventual base in Geneva, Calvin became one of the most influential leaders of the Protestant movement. His principles and church organization influenced the Protestant Reformation all over northern Europe.

These Protestant leaders went beyond changing the church practice. They also imposed a stricter way of life on their followers. Protestant ideals of morality forbade many amusements, like dancing, that were allowed among Roman Catholics. Church decoration was frowned on, and many beautiful altars were destroyed. Paintings in churches were covered over. Some have been discovered and restored in recent decades.

The central regions of Switzerland were more committed to the Roman Catholic Church, while the large cities in the north and west welcomed change. Greater conflict arose because the reformers wanted to force others to follow their new doctrine. Although the differences started out as religious, they quickly became political, and violence erupted among cantons. Switzerland was no longer fighting with other countries, but the war between Catholic and Protestant cantons inside Switzerland became bitter.

Unrest from the West

In the late 1700s, the French monarchy became bankrupt. The king wanted to raise taxes. The nobility resisted, and the French Revolution began. It proclaimed the modern ideas of liberty,

Honoring the Fallen

During the French Revolution, more than six hundred Swiss mercenaries died at the Tuileries Palace when they stood in defense of the French royalty while revolutionaries attacked. In 1820, a sculpture called the Lion Monument was carved into a rock in the Glacier Garden in Lucerne as a reminder of the terrible cost of war.

equality, and fraternity and spread them by military force. In 1799, French general Napoleon Bonaparte seized power in Paris and continued to spread the new ideas across Europe.

Swiss supporters of the new French Republic had established the Helvetic Republic in Switzerland in 1798. They tried to make Switzerland a unified nation, rather than a group of independent cantons. This did not last long, and Switzerland fell into civil war. In 1803, Napoleon Bonaparte, now French emperor, intervened and created a new Swiss

French forces clashed with the Russian army at the Second Battle of Zürich in 1799. Switzerland was the site of many battles during the era of Napoleon.

Confederation. The cantons of St. Gallen, Graubünden, Aargau, Thurgau, Ticino, and Vaud were added to the confederation.

The Swiss finally saw peace when Napoleon was overthrown by the other European nations. In 1815, the Congress of Vienna, which reorganized Europe at the end of the Napoleonic wars, officially recognized the Swiss Confederation as an independent country. This agreement was particularly important because it officially recognized Switzerland's political neutrality. At this time, the French cantons of Valais, Neuchâtel, and Geneva officially became part of the confederation as well.

By this time, industry had become important in Switzerland. It was a center of watchmaking and the manufacture of textiles. The watchmaking industry was centered in Geneva, but the textile industry was spread throughout the country. Suppliers would provide raw materials such as cotton, wool, and silk to farmers, who would spin it into thread and weave it into cloth.

A Swiss girl spins wool into thread.

The Merciful General

General Guillaume-Henri Dufour, remembered for his quick victory during the civil war of 1847, called the Sonderbund War, is particularly known for how he handled the victory. He ordered his troops not to kill anyone unless it was necessary; the lives of the injured opposing soldiers were spared. As a result, only about 150 soldiers were killed that day.

Dufour and another Swiss man named Jean-Henri Dunant cofounded the Red Cross, a humanitarian organization that provides medical care and other help to victims during times of war. Many sites nationwide are named after Dufour, as is the country's tallest mountain, Dufourspitze.

A Struggle for Unity

Switzerland faced the ongoing challenge of working as a united country. The Swiss people were separated by rugged terrain, different languages and customs, and varying religious beliefs. Each canton had its own army, currency, and laws. In much of the confederation civil liberties were limited, and the rulers were deeply conservative. In the 1830s, in many cantons, people began working for more say in their government. Liberal changes occurred in some cantons, while conservative reaction occurred in others. In 1841, the Protestant canton of Aargau moved to dissolve the Catholic monasteries. In response to these and other measures, in 1845, the seven predominantly Catholic cantons formed a defensive league called the Sonderbund.

In 1847, the Swiss Diet, the confederation's legislative body, declared that this sort of alliance was not allowed and must be dissolved. The diet also voted to expel the Jesuits, a religious group that Lucerne, a Catholic canton, had invited in to handle religious education in their region. A brief civil war erupted from these moves. As a result of the war, the Swiss realized that they had to protect the rights of Catholics.

This attempted revolt made it even more obvious than before that the central government needed to not only unify the cantons but also let them make their own decisions. With so many cultural differences between cantons, they had to

A meeting of the Swiss Diet in 1847. The Swiss Diet was dominated by the Protestant cantons.

Caring for the Wounded

In 1858, a business trip brought a young Swiss man named Jean-Henri Dunant to Solferino, Italy, just after a terrible battle had occurred there. He was shocked by what he saw. Twenty-three thousand soldiers lay on the battlefield, some dead, some dying, and many injured. He rallied the support of the nearby towns to form makeshift hospital tents and care for the men, with no concern for which side they had fought on.

Dunant was inspired by this experience to write the book *A Memory of Solferino*. This book talked about the terrible cost of war and the need for a neutral organization that would care for the wounded. The International Committee of the Red Cross was organized as a result of this book. Its first meeting took place in Geneva in 1863. In 1901, Dunant was awarded the first Nobel Peace Prize.

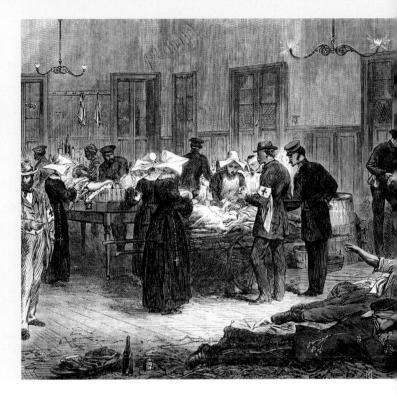

"agree to disagree." The result was the adoption of the first Swiss Federal Constitution, establishing the government structure, which was signed in 1848.

The constitution did not put an end to disagreements among cantons and various political and religious groups, but it set a framework for cooperation. In 1874, a new constitution was approved, which increased federal influence over the cantons.

Progress and Trade

As cooperation among the cantons increased, the national economy and infrastructure began to grow. By this time, Switzerland had become known for its high-quality products such as watches.

A big reason for Switzerland's success in trade was the construction of many rail lines. The Alps created a massive wall between northern and southern Europe, and although there were passes, they were still difficult to cross. Germany and Italy helped the Swiss cut a 9-mile (15 km) tunnel through solid rock. Called the St. Gotthard Pass, this tunnel opened in 1882 and was the first rail pass through the Alps. The construction of the railway line at St. Gotthard Pass was a major benefit not only for Switzerland but also for the rest of the continent, and it helped expand trade for many countries. By 1885, Switzerland had over 1,600 miles (2,575 km) of track and was the transportation hub of Europe.

The Swiss Army Knife

The world-famous Swiss Army knife did, in fact, begin as a standard issue tool for members of the Swiss Army. The tools began to be distributed to army members in 1891. The first batch of these clever folding multi-tools had actually been made in Germany, but by the end of 1891, they were being made in the little town of Ibach in Schwyz canton by a cutlery manufacturer named Karl Elsener. The original knife included a blade for cutting, a can opener, and a screwdriver that was used for rifle maintenance. In later years, models appeared that included additional blades, a corkscrew, a nail file, scissors, and many other tools. Modern hi-tech models include fingerprint scanners and USB storage with automatic data encryption. Today, more than fifteen million Swiss Army knives are sold every year.

A supply train passes through Neuchâtel during World War I.

War and Its Aftermath

In 1914, World War I began in Europe. In the war, the Central Powers—Germany, Austria-Hungary, Turkey, and others—were fighting a group of nations known as the Allies. These included France, Great Britain, Russia, and Italy. The United States entered the war on the side of Allies in 1917.

The war was a major test for Switzerland's neutrality. The Swiss army mobilized against attack from either side, but the country divided dangerously as German Swiss favored Germany and Austria and French Swiss favored the Allies. Italian Swiss remained neutral.

After the war ended in 1918, an international peace con-

ference was held in Paris. One outcome was that Switzerland agreed to protect Liechtenstein, its tiny neighbor. The Swiss took responsibility for the little country's defense, its customs regulations, and its international relationships. Another outcome of the conference was the creation of an international organization called the League of Nations. Because of Swiss neutrality, the league was established in Geneva.

Beginning in 1929, Switzerland suffered as a result of the worldwide economic crisis known as the Great Depression. People around the world stopped buying luxury goods such as Swiss watches, and Swiss exports collapsed. Many Swiss banks went out of business, and many workers lost their jobs.

By 1937, the economic situation was improving in Switzerland. But in many countries, the economic troubles of previous decades had contributed to the rise of antidemocratic and fascist governments. By 1932, most countries in central and eastern Europe were under the control of a dictatorship.

Europe in World War II, 1945

Neutral countries
Allied countries
Areas under Axis control

War Again

In 1939, war again spread across Europe. It had begun when Germany, under the control of Adolf Hitler and the Nazi Party,

Henri Guisan was the leader of the Swiss army during World War II. He was in charge of protecting Switzerland's independence during the war.

invaded neighboring Poland. Germany and its allies, Italy and Japan, were known as the Axis powers. Germany had already claimed Austria by the time the war started, and it soon gained control of France. This left Switzerland completely surrounded by lands under the control of the Axis powers. Switzerland again mobilized its army and awaited an Axis attack. Many Swiss leaders believed it would be best to give in to the Nazis because Switzerland was at such a large military disadvantage. But other Swiss stood firm.

General Henri Guisan was in charge of protecting the country. He was committed to putting up a strong resistance to any German invasion. In June 1940, he gave a speech to top-ranking Swiss officers. He proudly proclaimed his willingness to fight German expansion to the death. Rütli meadow, the site where he gave the speech, was highly symbolic because it was where the Swiss Confederation had begun in 1291. Guisan became a symbol of Swiss independence.

Even as Switzerland remained strictly neutral and allowed the Germans to use their mountain passes to reach Italy, the Swiss prepared for a possible attack. They made preparations along the passes so that, if necessary, their troops could mobi-

Hiding Under the Alps

During and after World War II, thousands of bunkers and other facilities were built in the Swiss mountains, connected by hundreds of tunnels. Some were used to house military equipment, ammunition, and troops. The Swiss even built hidden hangars for the air force, so planes could seemingly disappear right into the side of a mountain. The army hired artists and set designers to realistically camouflage the bunkers and outposts. Buildings that appear to be quaint, abandoned houses and barns were designed to hide cannons and other weapons. Today, enormous doors are still hidden in mountainsides, blending in with the surrounding rock. Many highways can be turned into runways quickly by removing the median separations. Exercises are still carried out using these runways, usually late at night. Many of the facilities, however, are no longer used by the military, because the threats to the country have changed. The bunkers under the mountains have been sold and converted into museums, restaurants, hotels, warehouses, and other businesses.

lize quickly and make every route impassable, freezing Nazi transportation. The Swiss were open about these plans, which worked to deter the Germans. Germany drew up plans to attack Switzerland but never dared risk it.

Unfortunately, an official stance of political neutrality did not prevent the Swiss from cooperating with the Nazis. The Nazis were systematically persecuting and murdering Jews, and in 1938, the Swiss government agreed to stop accepting Jewish refugees seeking escape from Austria, which the Nazis had just occupied. This led them to turn away tens of thou-

Bravery at the Border

In the 1930s, Germany became increasingly hostile to Jews. To escape the violence, many Jewish people left countries controlled by the Nazis, heading to places such as Switzerland (above).

Paul Grüninger was a police captain and head of border control in St. Gallen canton, on the Austrian border, during the Nazi occupation of Austria. In October 1938, the Nazis began stamping all Jewish passports with a J, and Switzerland agreed to not allow anyone with this stamp to cross the border. Anyone who was caught trying to illegally cross the border from Austria was brought to Captain Grüninger. But instead of following orders to send them back to the Nazis, Grüninger let them in the country. He not only let them in, he also forged their documents to make it look like they had arrived before the date of the agreement. This allowed them to be legal refugees and remain under the protection of Swiss law.

Despite warnings from friends that he was being watched by the Nazi police, Grüninger continued to help the refugees and even spent his own money buying them winter coats and supplies. On April 3, 1939, he was arrested after six months of helping Jews escape persecution. At the end of a two-year trial, he was found guilty of allowing 3,600 Jews to illegally enter the country, falsifying their documentation, and blocking investigations about illegal immigrants. He was also found guilty of breach of duty.

Grüninger spent the rest of his life in poverty, as an outcast because of his criminal record. The year before he died, in 1972, he was awarded a Medal of Honor by Yad Vashem, a Jewish organization. He holds the esteemed title of "Righteous Among the Nations." Since his death, the town of St. Gallen has renamed a public square after him, and many streets and other public places have been named in his honor. In 1995, Switzerland officially annulled the conviction.

sands of men, women, and children who were likely killed during the war.

Swiss banks, art dealers, and some individuals also profited from the spoils of war. All over Europe, Nazi troops pillaged homes, businesses, and banks, taking everything of value. They took what would now be worth billions of U.S. dollars. Money and gold stolen by the Nazis were deposited in secure Swiss banks, and valuables were put in safe deposit boxes. Artwork was bought by Swiss dealers and sold for profit. Swiss banks were also left with large deposits made by Jewish families before the war that were left unclaimed because the owners had died.

A self-portrait by Dutch artist Vincent van Gogh that had been seized by the Nazis is auctioned in Lucerne in 1939.

Swiss president Kaspar Villiger speaks at a ceremony at the United Nations headquarters in New York City in 2002, when Switzerland finally joined the organization.

After the War

In the years after the war, Switzerland maintained its strict neutrality. It refused to join many international organizations. It did not join the United Nations, an organization of nations founded in the aftermath of the war that is meant to promote peace, until 2002. Nor did it join the European Economic Community (EEC), a group of European nations working to promote economic growth. The EEC was a forerunner of today's European Union (EU), a political and economic union that includes most countries in Europe, but not Switzerland.

Rights for Women

Switzerland was one of the last countries in which women gained the right to vote at the federal level. The Swiss constitution cannot be changed without a vote of the people, and many Swiss men were reluctant to vote to allow women to join them at the polls.

The first official attempt to get voting laws changed was in 1886 when a group of women in Zürich petitioned without success. The first group dedicated solely to the cause was the Swiss Association for Women's Right to Vote, which formed in 1909. During the two world wars, the country's attention was elsewhere. It was not until 1959 that progress was finally made, when the cantons Vaud and Neuchâtel passed laws that allowed women to vote at the cantonal level. Geneva was the next, in 1960. Other cantons followed suit over the next few years.

The rest of Europe had given women voting rights many years before. Switzerland was eager to become a member of the European Convention on Human Rights, but it was decades behind other countries in giving its own female citizens rights. Between the pressure of allies and the number of cantons that had already decided in favor of voting rights for women, the federal government put the issue to vote. At last, on February

7, 1971, the men of Switzerland voted in favor of the women's right to vote. Later that same year, eleven women were elected as members of parliament.

The fight was not entirely over, however. Two conservative cantons, Appenzell Ausserrhoden and Appenzell Innerrhoden, refused to change their cantonal constitutions. It was not until 1991, following a federal court order, that Appenzell Innerrhoden changed a law that had forbidden women from voting at the canton level.

Women march through Zürich in 1963 to demand the right to vote in federal elections. Swiss men did not vote to give women the right to vote until 1971.

Changing Society

In the second half of the twentieth century, many immigrants began moving to Switzerland. By 2014, about 28 percent of the people living in Switzerland were foreign born. In addition, more than three hundred thousand foreigners commute every day from France, Italy, and Germany to work in Switzerland.

Some Swiss people resent the influence of immigrants on their country. An anti-immigrant party called the Swiss People's Party has become Switzerland's largest political party. In 2014, the Swiss people approved an initiative to curb immigration and limit the free movement of people from EU countries. Switzerland's relationship with its European neighbors remains an unsettled question.

A group of Muslim women in Zürich. Many Muslim immigrants moved to Switzerland in the 1990s. Most were Bosnians, Albanians, and Turks.

CHAPTER 5

Power to the People

SWITZERLAND'S GOVERNMENT IS UNIQUE. IT COMES the closest to direct democracy of any nation in the world. In addition to voting for legislators who are supposed to represent their interests in congress, Swiss citizens themselves routinely vote to change laws and the constitution. In Switzerland, the people are sovereign, meaning the ultimate power lies with them.

The basic structure of the Swiss government was borrowed from the U.S. Constitution when Switzerland's first federal constitution was written in 1848. Switzerland's most recent constitution went into effect in 2000. Like the United States, Switzerland has three branches of government: executive, legislative, and judicial.

Executive Branch

The executive branch is led by the Swiss Federal Council, which serves as both the head of government and the head of state. The council has seven members who are elected to four-year terms by the members of the Federal Assembly. Any Swiss citizen is eligible to be elected to the Federal Council, but usu-

The Flag

The national flag of Switzerland is a thick white cross on a red background. The origins of the flag reach far back in history. The canton of Schwyz began flying a red flag in the mid-1200s, and white crosses representing Christianity were worn by Swiss troops since the Battle of Laupen in 1339. In the 1800s, a flag with a white cross on a red background became a unifying symbol for the diverse group of cantons. Switzerland officially adopted the flag in 1889. It is one of only two national flags that are square.

ally they are members of the assembly or government officials at the canton level. The members of the Federal Council also function as the cabinet, with each one heading departments such as finance, foreign affairs, and justice and police.

Pioneering President

Ruth Dreifuss can claim several firsts in the Swiss government. In 1993, she became the first woman elected to the Federal Council. In 1999, she became its first female president. She is also the first person of Jewish background to serve on the Federal Council. Dreifuss had worked as a journalist, a social worker, and an expert on development and humanitarian aid before joining the government in 1981 as an official in the Swiss Federal Trade Union.

As a member of the government, Dreifuss has been active in reforming federal regulations concerning social security and health care. She is also an advocate for women's rights and was instrumental in passing the 2004 legislation guaranteeing paid maternity leave.

The Federal Assembly also selects members of the Federal Council to be president and vice president for one-year terms. Essentially, the titles rotate through the members of the council. The duties of these positions are mainly ceremonial. They have no additional power on the council.

The members of the Federal Council raise their hands as they are sworn in during a meeting of the Federal Assembly.

Legislative Branch

Switzerland's legislative branch of government consists of the Federal Assembly. Like the U.S. Congress, the Federal Assembly has two houses. The upper house, called the Council of States, has forty-six members who are elected to four-year terms. Like the U.S. Senate, it gives equal representation to each of the cantons, regardless of their specific population. Most cantons are allotted two members, except for six small ones that have only one. The lower house, called

A meeting of the National Council. Its members represent more than a dozen different political parties.

the National Council, has two hundred members who serve four-year terms. As in the U.S. House of Representatives, in the National Council each canton receives a number of seats in proportion to its population.

A Look at the Capital

Bern was founded in 1191 as capital of its canton of the same name. Legend says that the city's founder, Berthold von Zähringen, caught a bear when hunting in the area and named the city after this conquest. The name Bern is related to the German word for "bear." Since 1513, the city has kept bears as mascots. It was chosen as the capital of Switzerland in 1848 and since then has housed most of the nation's federal offices.

Bern is located on the river Aare in west-central Switzerland. The city's population was about 130,000 in 2014. About 24 percent of the population consists of permanent foreign residents, and more than half of these are immigrants from EU countries.

A large portion of Bern's Old Town dates to the Middle Ages. This includes the Zytglogge clock tower,

which features figures that move when the clock chimes. It is also home to the Münster, a gothic cathedral on which construction began in 1421 and wasn't finished until 1893. Another popular site is the Albert Einstein House, where the scientist lived while he wrote his theory of relativity. Newer buildings in Bern include the Federal Palace, where the parliament meets, which was constructed in 1902. In addition, Bern has galleries, museums, and theaters that reflect both its rich history and its modern edge.

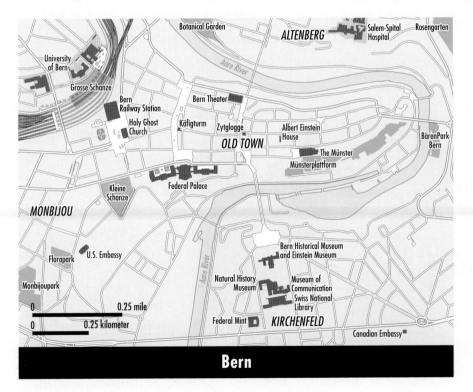

Bern

Every Swiss citizen is automatically registered to vote at age eighteen. Cantons set their own rules about voting. For example, the canton Glarus allows sixteen- and seventeen-year-olds to vote on issues and candidates at the canton level. The cantons of Jura and Neuchâtel allow foreign national residents to vote in both canton and commune elections. Other cantons allow communes within them to grant foreign residents voting rights if they so desire. Foreign residents are not allowed to vote in the federal elections.

Direct Representation

Citizens participate in a direct democracy three to four times a year on various issues at different levels of government. Some decisions must be put before the people. These are called referendums because they are "referred" to the people. Swiss citizens vote on amendments to the constitution and on international treaties. Laws can also be reversed by a referendum. For a challenge to a law to be put on a ballot, fifty thousand signatures must be collected within one hundred days of the law being passed.

Swiss people must first gather signatures to put an initiative on a ballot. Here, people deliver boxes of signatures collected in support of an initiative to end Switzerland's military draft.

Swiss citizens can also propose laws through initiatives. An initiative begins with a petition that must be signed by one hundred thousand eligible voters within eighteen months. The proposal is then reviewed by the government and put on a ballot. Over the years, the Swiss people

Switzerland's National Government

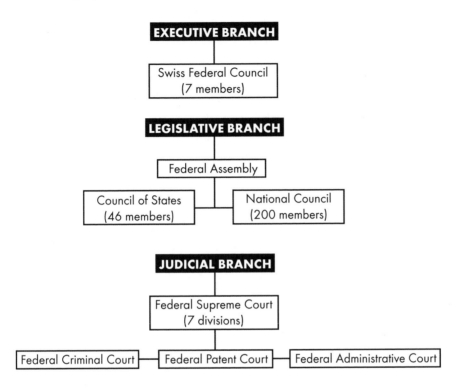

have voted directly on many vital issues, including granting women the right to vote, and eliminating the military, an idea that was rejected.

Regional and Local Government

Switzerland is made up of twenty-six cantons. Each canton has a great deal of authority and has its own constitution. Separations caused by language, culture, and geographic barriers mean that the needs and the wants of each region's residents can be very different. Because of this, the Swiss believe it is important for each group to be able to make their own laws and deal with issues in their own way. Each canton

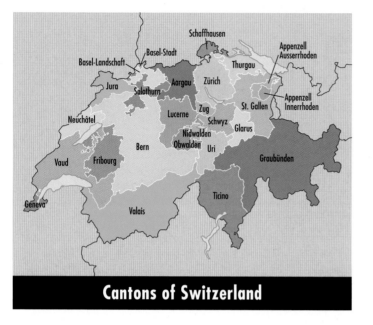

Cantons of Switzerland

has its own executive, parliament, and court system. The officials are elected by a popular vote. Each canton is responsible for its own education system, roadways, and social services.

Judicial Branch

The highest court in Switzerland is the Federal Supreme Court, which is located in Lausanne. Thirty-eight judges organized in seven divisions sit on the Federal Supreme Court. Each division deals with a different type of law, such as criminal law or social law, which includes accident insurance. The court also deals with issues such as international law and inter-cantonal law. Federal Supreme Court judges are elected by the Federal Assembly to six-year terms.

Other federal courts include the Federal Criminal Court, which covers only federal crimes, the Federal Patent Court, and the Federal Administrative Court. Most cases are handled at the canton level. Each canton has its own trial courts and supreme court.

Cantons are divided into districts, which are further divided into communes. Each commune is responsible for its own public services such as police and fire protection, and maintaining the infrastructure like local roads and bridges.

National Anthem

Switzerland's national anthem, "Schweizerpsalm" or "Swiss Psalm," was written in 1841 by Albert Zwyssig. Although the song was frequently performed at events, it was not named the official anthem until 1981.

German lyrics

Trittst im Morgenrot daher,

Seh' ich dich im Strahlenmeer,

Dich, du Hocherhabener, Herrlicher!

Wenn der Alpenfirn sich rötet,

Betet, freie Schweizer betet!

Eure fromme Seele ahnt,

Gott im hehren Vaterland,

Gott, den Herrn, im hehren Vaterland.

Italian lyrics

Quando bionda aurora

il mattin c'indora

l'alma mia t'adora re del ciel!

Quando l'alpe già rosseggia

a pregare allor t'atteggia;

in favor del patrio suol,

cittadino Iddio lo vuol,

cittadino Dio, si Dio lo vuol.

French lyrics

Sur nos monts, quand le soleil

Annonce un brillant réveil,

Et prédit d'un plus beau jour le retour,

Les beautés de la patrie

Parlent à l'âme attendrie;

Au ciel montent plus joyeux

Les accents d'un cœur pieux,

Les accents émus d'un cœur pieux.

English translation

When the morning skies grow red

And over us their radiance shed

Thou, O Lord, appeareth in their light!

When the Alps glow bright with splendor,

Pray to God, to Him surrender!

For you feel and understand

That God dwelleth in this land.

That God, the Lord, dwelleth in this land.

CHAPTER 6

Quality and Care

Throughout the world, Switzerland is known for the high quality of its products. Its watches are renowned for their precision and its chocolate for its perfect texture and flavor. Swiss products are sometimes expensive, but they are trusted for their high standards.

What Switzerland Grows, Makes, and Mines

AGRICULTURE

Sugar beets (2013)	1,376,000 metric tons
Wheat (2012)	515,595 metric tons
Cattle (2013)	1,563,214 animals

MANUFACTURING (PERCENTAGE OF EXPORTS, 2014)

Chemicals	41%
Machinery and electronic equipment	16%
Watches	11%

MINING (2012)

Salt	528,000 metric tons
Gypsum	320,000 metric tons

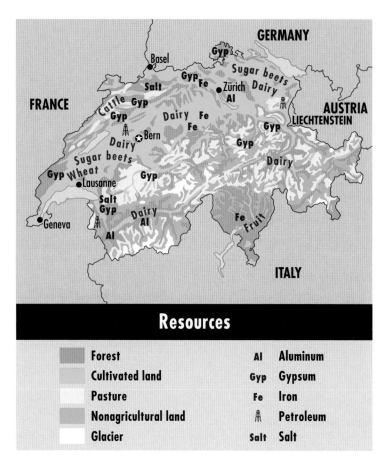

Resources

	Forest		
	Cultivated land	Al	Aluminum
	Pasture	Gyp	Gypsum
	Nonagricultural land	Fe	Iron
	Glacier	⛏	Petroleum
		Salt	Salt

From the Land

Agriculture is the smallest portion of the economy, employing only about 3 percent of the people. But even Swiss who have lived in the city their entire lives feel close to the land and consider agriculture an important part of their national heritage.

Switzerland's small size and large areas of mountain terrain make it difficult for the Swiss to produce enough food for everyone in the country. About 60 percent of the food consumed in Switzerland is produced there. The remainder is imported.

The biggest farm crops in Switzerland are sugar beets; cereal grains such as wheat, barley, and oats; potatoes; and plants for oil production like rapeseed and sunflower. Christmas trees are also a growing industry, especially in areas where traditional crops are more difficult to grow. In southern Switzerland, berries and other fruits are grown.

Livestock accounts for more than half of the farming industry, and about 20 percent of Swiss grain crops are used to feed these animals. Common farm animals in Switzerland include chickens, goats, pigs, sheep, and dairy cattle. Of all

A picture of Alpine meadows with snow-covered mountain peaks beyond often shows brown Swiss cows grazing contentedly in the foreground. You can almost hear the cowbells in the morning air!

Several different breeds are typically Swiss, and each region has its own customs and even festivals surrounding their local cows. In the Valais, the mountain region east of Geneva, the black Hérens breed thrives at high altitudes. It is not a placid and peaceful animal. These cows fight each other every spring, locking horns and pushing until one has to step back. This determines which will be the queen cow, leading the herd up to the alpine meadows. Popular festivals bring these queens together for the crowning of village and regional champions.

Throughout Switzerland, towns have spring festivals when the herds are moved up to graze on the rich green pastures and meadows in the mountains. Children in traditional costumes parade through the streets with the cows, which are often decorated with crowns of flowers and fancy embroidered collars.

the animal products, milk makes the most money for farmers. Over a third of the milk produced is used to make cheese, while only a little over 10 percent ends up as drinking milk. Swiss farms supply almost all the domestic dairy needs, and provide cheese for export.

Industry

About 23 percent of Swiss workers are employed in industry. Switzerland has long been known for its precision manufacturing,

Keeping Time

The Swiss watch industry dates back to the 1500s. Geneva was a center for goldsmiths and jewelers until 1541, when the religious reformer John Calvin banned wearing jewelry or other ornaments. The industry adapted by turning to making watches, which could be decorative yet functional, so they didn't break this law. The first watchmaker in Geneva was a French emigrant named Thomas Bayard. Exiled for religious reasons, French watchmakers continued to settle in Geneva as its reputation as a watchmaking capital grew.

In 1601, the first organization of its kind, the Watchmakers Guild of Geneva, was established. Over the next century, the city's watchmaking industry grew so much that the craftsmen began to move their shops to towns, spreading north throughout the Jura region. By 1700, the industry and its related jobs dominated the entire region's economy. And by 1830, the watchmaking industry employed nearly one-quarter of the population of Geneva.

In the centuries that followed, the Swiss watchmaking industry was challenged by foreign innovation, trade restrictions, and other issues. In the 1980s, the Swatch brand reintroduced Swiss watches to the world and helped revive the industry, which is today very strong.

building goods such as motors. The country is particularly known for its high-quality watches, one of its most valuable exports.

Switzerland also has a large pharmaceutical industry, which develops and manufactures medicines. The nation is home to some of the world's largest pharmaceutical companies, including Novartis and Hoffmann-La Roche. Basel is a center of the industry. About fifty thousand people in the

A worker monitors the production of medicine at a factory in Basel.

Sweet Innovation

In 1863, the candle maker Daniel Peter married Fanny Cailler, the daughter of the owners of the Cailler chocolate company. Gaslights were beginning to replace candles, and Peter began thinking about a new career. He had some ideas about chocolate that he thought could help with his family's company, but they declined his offer. He was convinced that he could innovate the business, though, and took a temporary job in a chocolate factory to learn about the process. He researched every step of chocolate production, down to the growth of the bean itself.

After years of experimentation and failed results, Daniel finally developed a way to mix milk with chocolate so that it would not separate or go bad. He named this first solid milk chocolate Gala. It became popular, and in 1904 his company joined forces with the Kohler

Chocolate Company. Together, they formed the Société Générale Suisse de Chocolats, which sold their goods internationally under the Nestlé name. Today, Swiss chocolate is the gold standard to which all other chocolates are compared.

region are employed in the pharmaceutical and other health technology industries.

Mining is almost nonexistent in Switzerland. Salt is the most common product mined in the country. Gypsum, a mineral with many uses in industry, is also taken from the ground.

Service Industries

About 71 percent of Swiss workers are employed in service industries. Jobs in stores, restaurants, hotels, transportation, education, banking, and health care are all part of the service sector of the economy.

Banking is the most valuable industry in Switzerland. Nationally, there are more than three hundred banks, most

of which have multiple branches. The two largest banks are Credit Suisse and UBS (Union Bank of Switzerland). Swiss banks are known worldwide for their secrecy. Because of their extremely strict confidentiality laws, they gained a reputation for being the best place to keep money safely. In recent years, however, many Swiss banks have been investigated because they have been used for money laundering and tax evasion. The banks have been fined billions of dollars, and Switzerland has lost some prestige as a result.

Tourism is another major service industry in Switzerland. People come from near and far to hike, ski, and explore Switzerland's beautiful cities and towns.

Money Facts

The Swiss franc is the official currency of Switzerland. Just as one hundred pennies make up a dollar in the United States and Canada, one hundred centimes equals one franc. Coins are available in 5, 10, 20, and 50 centimes, and 1, 2, and 5 francs. Paper currency comes in denominations of 10, 20, 50, 100, 200, and 1,000 francs.

The bills show a prominent Swiss cultural figure on the front and an image of the person's work on the back. Each denomination of bill also has a different main color. For example, the 10-franc note is primarily yellow. The front has an image of the architect Le Corbusier, while the back shows one of his plans. In 2016, 1 Swiss franc was worth US$1.03, and US$1.00 equaled 0.97 francs.

Melting Pot

SWITZERLAND IS A DIVERSE PLACE. IT HAS FOUR official languages, each associated with its own ethnic group and geographical region of the country. Cultures may be different and opinions may be in conflict, but the Swiss manage to live together in harmony despite their differences.

Who Lives in Switzerland?

The 2014 census counted approximately 8,237,700 permanent residents in the country of Switzerland. Of these, less than 25 percent are not Swiss natives. Instead, they are classified as permanent foreign residents. The largest number of

Opposite: **People fill a pedestrian street in Bern. About one out of every five residents of Bern was born outside of Switzerland.**

Population of Major Cities (2014 est.)	
Zürich	391,400
Geneva	194,600
Basel	168,600
Lausanne	133,900
Bern	130,000

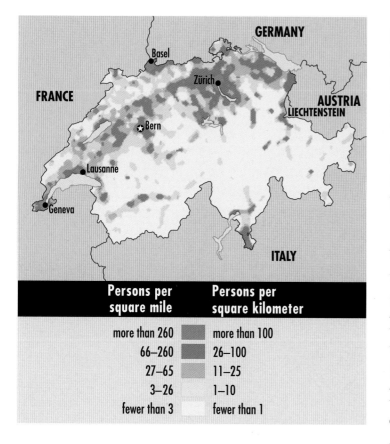

Persons per square mile	Persons per square kilometer
more than 260	more than 100
66–260	26–100
27–65	11–25
3–26	1–10
fewer than 3	fewer than 1

Switzerland's Languages (2014)

German	63.3%
French	22.7%
Italian	8.1%
English	4.6%
Portuguese	3.6%
Albanian	3.0%
Serbian/Croatian	2.5%
Spanish	2.2%
Rumantsch	0.5%

foreign residents comes from Italy, followed by Germany and Portugal. There are also many people from France, Serbia, Turkey, and Spain. In recent decades, Switzerland's population has been growing, primarily because of immigration.

More than four out of every five people in Switzerland live in urban areas. The country, splintered by the steep mountains, has abundant small cities and towns. Many of the major cities, including Zürich, Geneva, and Lucerne, are located at the end of lakes. This allowed them to grow as transportation hubs. In recent years, sprawl has emerged around some of these cities.

Land of Many Voices

Most countries have one or two official languages, but Switzerland has four: German, French, Italian, and Rumantsch. German is the primary language of about two-thirds of the population, and French is spoken by a little more than one-fifth of the residents. Italian is spoken by a little less than one-tenth of the population. Rumantsch is an old regional language used by only half a percent of Swiss. All product

labels, instructions, and official documents are required by law to be provided in the three major languages, no matter where in the country they are sold.

The form of German that is spoken in Switzerland is different from the language spoken in Germany or Austria. While its written form is the same, Swiss German includes many different dialects that vary from region to region. These forms

Members of the United Nations Human Rights Council discuss a resolution concerning violence in Syria. The organization meets in Geneva.

are so different that people who speak one dialect cannot be understood by those who speak another dialect.

French Swiss speak standard French with an accent. French-speaking Switzerland is in the west, near the border with France. The line between the French- and German-speaking areas is called Röstigraben, which literally means "fried potatoes ditch." As silly as this name sounds, it refers to the way the local food traditions reflect the language and cultural differences. *Rösti* is a popular fried potato dish in German-speaking Switzerland.

A sign in a Swiss park says "thank you" in German, French, and Italian.

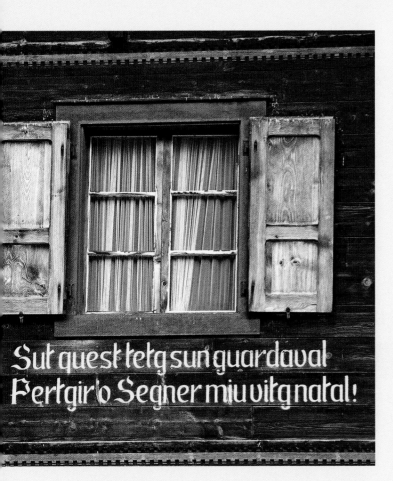

Rumantsch, also known as Romansch, is an old language unique to a few small areas of Switzerland. It has its roots in Latin, just as French and Italian do. Because of this, many Rumantsch words may look similar to words in French and Italian, but pronunciation is sometimes very different. Except for in a few isolated towns, business everywhere is conducted in one of the other dominant languages, so Rumantsch is being spoken less and less. An organization called Lia Rumantscha tries to keep this unique language alive in hopes of saving it from extinction and preserving the traditions of old Switzerland.

Rumantsch is one of the official languages of the canton Graubünden, and is also spoken in parts of the Rhine Valley and the Engadin region. All of these are tucked within the predominantly German-speaking area. Since so few people actually speak Rumantsch, those who grow up in these areas also learn Swiss German and are completely bilingual. About half of the country's Rumantsch speakers live in Zürich, but they all speak Swiss German in their daily lives.

The border symbolizes more than just a language change. There is a cultural shift, viewed as the place where the old meets the new. Many Swiss view the German-speaking residents as more conservative and traditional, while the French-speaking Swiss are considered to lean toward more liberal, forward-thinking views.

The Italian-speaking region is in southern Switzerland, surrounded on three sides by Italy. Italian is the official language

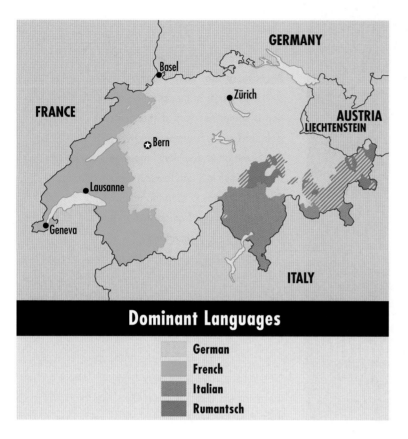

Dominant Languages

- German
- French
- Italian
- Rumantsch

of the canton Ticino, and is also spoken in the western region of the canton Graubünden. Just as French culture and foods predominate in French cantons, the Italian way of life is evident in the Ticino. Even the houses look more like those in Italy, and towns have more of a Mediterranean feel.

Knowledge Is Power

Switzerland prides itself in having an excellent public education system. Each canton is responsible for its own schools, so the programs and requirements vary from place to place. This includes differences in the age children begin school, the language the classes are taught in, and which other languages are taught. This can make moving from one canton to another especially difficult for families with children in school.

Preschool is called *Kindergarten*, a German word that was adopted by North Americans for the similar grade level. The next level is called *Volksschule*, roughly the same as elementary school and middle school combined. In most areas, this is split into two segments. After Volksschule, students must choose between *Berufslehre*, an apprenticeship, or *Gymnasium*, secondary school, which is similar to high school in the United States.

The Swiss take education very seriously and view it as an extremely important element of their society. Swiss students are required to learn at least two languages, although some cantons require more.

Several students watch another work at a school in Geneva.

Four Languages, One Country

English: Switzerland
German: *Schweiz*
French: *Suisse*
Italian: *Svizzera*
Rumantsch: *Svizra*

English: Hi
German: *Gruezi*
French: *Salut*
Italian: *Ciao*
Rumantsch: *Tgau*

English: Good-bye
German: *Auf Wiedersehen*
French: *Au revoir*
Italian: *Arrivederci*
Rumantsch: *Sin seveser*

English: Thank you
German: *Danke*
French: *Merci*
Italian: *Grazie*
Rumantsch: *Engraziel*

Berufslehre is hands-on training in a trade or technical occupation. It prepares the students for their chosen career by giving them real-life experience. Once done with the apprenticeship, students have the option of going on to a university of applied sciences to advance academically in their chosen field, such as engineering or architecture. Both Gymnasium and Berufslehre students have the option of going on to a college or university.

A Berufslehre student observes an experienced worker in Thurgau canton, in northern Switzerland.

The University of Basel, founded in 1460, is the country's oldest university. The University of Geneva was founded in 1559. All but two of the country's universities are operated and funded by the cantons. Those two, the Swiss Federal Institute of Technology in Zürich and the Swiss Federal Institute of Technology in Lausanne, are federally managed and focus on technology. They are among the top science and engineering schools in the world.

Young people study at the library of the Law Institute at the University of Zürich. With twenty-six thousand students, the University of Zürich is Switzerland's largest university.

CHAPTER 8

Spiritual Life

MANY DIFFERENT CULTURES LONG AGO MOVED through or settled on the land that is now Switzerland. Each group—the Celtic Helvetii, Romans, Germanic tribes, early Christians, and others—brought their own beliefs that grew into local folklore. Today, in most places, the creatures and spirits of the old tales have become the subjects of children's stories or lively parts of festivals.

Some of these mythical Swiss creatures are good and others are not. The Barbegazi are said to be small furry men with large feet. They are shy and rarely seen but are helpful and make magical cheese from the milk of the herds they tend in the mountains. On January 2, several places in Switzerland celebrate Berchtoldstag. The name of this holiday has several possible origins. One is that it is in honor of Berchta, a white-robed Germanic goddess who leads her band of Berchten to drive away evil spirits. Some of the most curious folklore

Opposite: **Lausanne Cathedral was built in the 1200s. It is one of Switzerland's greatest gothic churches, with soaring ceilings and beautiful stained glass windows.**

creatures are made up of parts from different animals. The tall Schnabelgeiss has goat horns and a beak, and the Tatzelwurm is half cat and half snake.

Christianity

The arrival of Christianity in what is now Switzerland dates back more than 1,500 years. St. Maurice d'Augune, one of the

Masked figures march in the Berchtoldstag parade in Interlaken, a town near Bern. The creatures are said to scare away winter.

oldest monasteries in Europe, was founded in Valais Canton in 515 CE. The Abbey of St. Gall, in St. Gallen in northeastern Switzerland, was founded in the 700s and became an important center of learning.

Switzerland was Roman Catholic until the Protestant Reformation of the 1500s. Traditionally, central and southern Switzerland were Catholic, and the regions near the larger cities such as Zürich, Geneva, and Basel were Protestant. Over time, however, the regions became much more mixed.

Today, about 38 percent of Swiss are Roman Catholic, and 33 percent are Protestant. Switzerland does not have a national religion, but the cantons recognize official churches. These include the Roman Catholic Church and the Federation of

Swiss Protestant Churches. These churches are supported by taxes that are paid by their members.

Most Protestants belong to the Swiss Reformed Church, which traces its origins back to the Reformation of the 1500s. This is not one church with one consistent set of beliefs, or theology. Instead, each church in each canton expresses its own theology and has its own organization. A small number of Swiss belong to other Protestant groups, including Baptists, Lutherans, and Pentecostals.

John Calvin frequently preached in what is now called the Calvin Auditorium, in Geneva. Like other Swiss Reformed churches, the chapel is simple, with little decoration.

Islam

In recent decades, the number of Muslims, followers of the religion Islam, has grown in Switzerland. Most of this increase is the result of immigration from Turkey or southeastern Europe. Muslims now make up about 5 percent of Switzerland's population.

Some Swiss dislike the growing number of Muslims in Switzerland. In a national referendum in 2009, 58 percent of voters approved a proposal outlawing the construction of minarets, the towers that are attached to mosques, Muslim houses of worship. Many Swiss officials believe the ban is contrary to the right to freedom of religion, which is enshrined in the Swiss Constitution, but the ban remains in effect.

Swiss Muslims pray at a mosque in Lucerne. Muslims stop whatever they are doing to pray five times a day.

Religion in Switzerland (2013)	
Roman Catholic	38%
Swiss Reformed	26%
Other Christian	6%
Muslim	5%
Other	2%
Unaffiliated	22%
Unknown	1%

Religious Holidays

Good Friday	March or April
Easter	March or April
Ascension Day	May
Whit Monday	May
Corpus Christi	Late May or June
Assumption Day	August
All Saints' Day	November 1
Christmas	December 25
St. Stephen's Day	December 26

Traditions Old and New

Although most Swiss belong to a church, many do not attend services on a regular basis. It is estimated that about 40 percent of Catholics and 50 percent of Protestants attend church regularly.

But even families that do not go to church regularly often choose to observe major events with a church ceremony. The baptism of a baby varies depending on the family's religion, so there is no single custom that is followed everywhere. Families usually have a party following a baptism, and guests bring gifts for the baby. One old tradition is to plant a tree in the baby's honor.

Weddings in Switzerland, as in many European countries, must begin with a legal ceremony at a registry office. After this, the couple can choose to be married in a church or somewhere else. In the summer, many couples have their wedding in a mountain chapel or at a scenic spot in the Alps. Most brides dress in white and follow a few old traditions, like wearing a crown of flowers. Riding in a horse-drawn carriage is another old tradition that is popular today.

As many Swiss have moved away from church practices, they are finding new ways to show respect for relatives who have died. Many families scatter ashes in the forest or in a favorite spot of the person who died. In the same way, funeral services are changing, reflecting different spiritual beliefs. But whatever a family's beliefs, friends gather to remember the person who has died and share the family's grief.

A couple signs their marriage certificate at a Catholic church in Switzerland.

CHAPTER 9

Culture
and Sports

ART AND SPORTS ARE CENTRAL TO LIFE IN Switzerland. Zürich alone has more than a dozen art museums, and every city has at least one concert hall. Each summer, Montreux, a city on Lake Geneva, hosts one of the world's largest jazz festivals, and the Lucerne Festival draws more than one hundred thousand music lovers. Swiss love the outdoors and sports in all seasons. Switzerland attracts skiers from all over the world and has twice hosted the Winter Olympics.

Opposite: **Many buildings in Switzerland, both old and new, are painted with murals.**

Folk Art Traditions

Poya painting is a traditional form of mural art found in the Alpine regions. The word *poya* refers to an entire event—a farmer's ascent to the grazing pastures with his herd. The paintings were traditionally done on the side of a farmhouse or barn, showing the farmer, his workers, and all of the livestock as they

Creating with Scissors

Cutting connected rows of paper snowflakes or paper dolls has its origin in a traditional Swiss handcraft. It's called *scherenschnitte*, or scissor cuts, and it is such a fine art that framed scherenschnitte pictures are sold for high prices in art galleries. Skilled artists make intricate scenes and designs using very sharp, tiny scissors. Often they are cut from a folded sheet so that the two halves are identical when unfolded.

You can make a Swiss chalet, or wooden cottage, from a folded sheet of colored paper (thin paper works better than thick construction paper). Draw one half of the chalet on the paper, with the point of the roof right on the fold. To make it look like a chalet, leave a long overhang at the lower edge of the roof. Cut out windows and doors. You might want to add a balcony to the outside wall. Be as detailed as you like or keep your chalet simple. You can even refold it and add more details after you've opened and looked at it. To finish your scherenschnitte, glue it very lightly to white paper.

climb to the fresh fields. Modern poya painters have found markets in interior design and commissioned work for collectors.

A type of folk art called Bauernmalerei has been around since the 1500s. These paintings of rural life and flower designs are done on smaller items, from chairs and tables to milk pails, ladders, and window boxes. "Peasant" ceramics also have these themes, traditionally done as pictures of each farm's prize livestock and land. The Brienz Woodcarving School teaches the art of making intricate woodcarvings as well as basket making and other artistic woodworking.

Modern Art and Architecture

Basel is considered a major art center in Switzerland. In the early 1900s, it was a popular place for artists in the constructivism movement, which brought an appreciation of machines, technology, and geometry to visual arts. The combination of art and precision is a theme that is found throughout Swiss creativity.

This is especially true of the country's architects such as Le Corbusier. A leader in the modern movement in architecture in the early twentieth century, he was known for his pure, functional work that incorporated concrete and steel. He designed many housing units and other buildings in France and Switzerland as well as several government buildings in Chandigarh, India. Switzerland honored Le Corbusier's contribution by depicting him on the 10-franc bill.

Le Corbusier looks at a model of a building. His work emphasized both function and bold design.

Mixing Man and Machine

H. R. Giger was born in 1940 in Chur, a small city in eastern Switzerland. From a young age, he was fascinated by the morbid and bizarre. His schooling took him to Zürich, where he studied architecture and worked in interior design. His focus quickly changed, however, and he soon became a fine artist. In the 1970s, he began to use an airbrush to create intense detailed work showing humans with industrial elements. Some of his best-known works are the creatures in the film *Alien*, for which he earned an Oscar in 1980. He also contributed to the later *Alien* films, as well as *Poltergeist II* and *Species*. Today, his work is displayed in many museums, including in the H. R. Giger Museum in Gruyères.

Folk Music

The long alpenhorn is one of the symbols of Switzerland. It was first used so that Swiss could be heard over long distances from mountain to mountain. Like yodeling, another Swiss musical tradition, it was used by Alpine herders to communicate with people in the villages below. The strong deep tone of the alpenhorn, like the sudden pitch changes of yodeling, makes the sound carry farther. Both yodeling and the alpenhorn became part of Switzerland's folk music tradition.

They had almost died out, however, by the 1800s, when there was a reawakening of national pride and nostalgia for traditions from the past. The sounds of both became popular at festivals and soon the Swiss Yodeling Association was

Master Artist

Paul Klee, one of the greatest artists of the twentieth century, was born in Münchenbuchsee, near Bern, in 1879. His parents were both musicians, but he didn't care for popular music so he began to draw as a way to express his creativity. When he was nineteen he enrolled in the Academy of Fine Arts in Munich, Germany. He was talented in drawing, but didn't feel like he would ever be a good painter. When he returned to Bern he experimented with several techniques, including etching and inscribing on blackened glass with a needle. His first solo exhibit was in Bern in 1910.

The following year in Munich he and other artists joined to form the Blue Rider group. The members of this group wanted to use art as a form of spiritual expression. They were part of a major artistic movement called expressionism.

In the 1930s, Nazi leaders in Germany condemned the expressionist painters for their abstract pictures. Their works in museums were destroyed. Klee and his family moved back to Switzerland in late 1933. He continued to work until his death in Locarno in 1940.

He left the world a legacy of more than nine thousand works of art. He is best known for his works that combine geometric shapes, especially colored rectangles and circles, with simple line figures.

formed for both yodelers and alpenhorn players to preserve these traditions. Yodeling is popular in its original folk music form, but has also been incorporated into more modern popular music.

Alpenhorns are made of wood. Many of them reach 12 feet (4 m) in length.

Although people perfect yodeling only after a lot of practice, almost anyone can learn to yodel. The trick is to change very quickly from very low notes to a very high-pitched sound. The basic refrain is "Yodel-ay-EEE–oooo" with the "EEE" sung in a very high voice.

Sports

Traditional Swiss sports focus on strength and physical fitness. Swiss wrestling is called *Schwingen* (meaning "to swing"

Swiss wrestlers traditionally wear shorts, made of a type of coarse thread called jute, over their clothes.

in German). The object of the match is to get the opponent's shoulders to touch the ground by grabbing the waist of his pants and throwing him down. Traditionally, the prizes for winning championships are cattle and other livestock.

Steinstossen is just what it sounds like—stone tossing. It is one of the oldest competition sports, first recorded in the 1200s in Basel. Steinstossen is like the shot-put event in track-and-field competitions, but the stone is larger. At the Unspunnen Festival in Interlaken, the stone weighs 184 pounds (84 kilograms).

Alpine Skiing

Snow blankets the mountains of Switzerland in the winter. Traditionally, for mountain people, traveling through the snow was a necessity, not a sport. People typically used snowshoes.

Hotel owner Johannes Badrutt had no trouble getting wealthy British families to stay in the Alpine town of St. Moritz during the summer, when the fresh mountain air was a welcome relief from the heat of London, England. But his hotel stood empty in the winter even though St. Moritz was warmer than London. So in 1864, he challenged his summer guests to spend a week with him in winter, promising that if they didn't like it, he would pay for their stay. Four families came for Christmas, and they were so delighted that soon St. Moritz was as busy in the winter as in the summer. Other Alpine towns began welcom-

A steinstossen competitor heaves a stone at the Unspunnen Festival in Interlaken.

ing winter guests, who enjoyed outdoor sports such as sled races, tobogganing, snowshoeing, and ice-skating.

Skis were not common in those years. When they were used, it was for work, not play. By 1893, skis were given to some mail carriers, and the military was using them when guarding the St. Gotthard Pass. But it didn't take long for people to realize the thrill of sliding down mountains at high speed. In

A string quartet plays for skaters at the St. Moritz resort in 1924.

Down the Mountain

Ski racer Dominique Gisin was born in Engelberg, Switzerland, in 1985, and in 2005, competed in her first race in the World Cup, the world's premier skiing competition. She won her first World Cup race in 2009. But the most thrilling moment of her career took place at the 2014 Winter Olympics when she tied Tina Maze of Slovenia for first place in the downhill competition. They were both awarded gold medals. Never before had there been a tie for gold in an Olympic alpine event.

1904 the first ski jumping competition was held in St. Moritz, and in 1911 the first organized downhill ski classic, the Roberts of Kandahar Challenge Cup, was held on a glacier in Crans-Montana, Switzerland.

Swiss soldiers train on skis in 1946. Even today, Switzerland has a group of soldiers who work on skis in the mountains.

Cable cars carry skiers up many of the mountains in Switzerland.

Today, skiing is one of the biggest parts of Swiss tourism, and the Swiss Alps have some of the world's most famous ski resorts. Skiers from all over the world dream of skiing the Matterhorn, and St. Moritz remains a popular resort.

Olympic Games

The International Olympic Committee has its headquarters in Lausanne. The committee coordinates all the organizations that are responsible for making the Olympics happen. This includes each country's Olympic committee, host city organizing committees, broadcasting networks, and many other groups.

This organization was started in 1894 by a historian named Pierre de Coubertin. He had a lifelong fascination with ancient Greece, where the Olympic Games were first held, and wanted to revive them. He believed that the games would help different cultures move past their differences. Today, the Olympics remain a symbol of international unity, and to many people it makes sense that they are based in Switzerland, a neutral country. Switzerland has hosted the Olympic games twice, in 1928 and 1948, both times at St. Moritz.

Throughout the history of the Olympics, Swiss athletes have performed well in both summer and winter games. As of 2015, they had won 185 medals at the Summer Games, and 138 at the Winter Games, including 59 medals in Alpine skiing.

Roger Federer is considered one of the greatest tennis players ever. He has twice represented Switzerland at the Olympic Games.

CHAPTER 10

Swiss Life

Everyday life for families in Switzerland is much the same as it is in the United States or Canada. During the week, people go to school and work. Weekends mean more time for family activities and sports. For farm families, children may spend more time helping with animals and other chores on the weekends.

Day by Day

Although each canton sets its own school hours, most children are in school from about 8:00 a.m. until noon and from 2:00 until 4:00 p.m. Most children go home for lunch, but those who remain at school for lunch can play sports when they're not eating. There is no school on Wednesday afternoons. After school and on weekends, many students go to local sports clubs or to meetings of the Swiss Guides and Scouts, the Swiss version of the Boy Scouts and Girl Scouts.

Family Facts

An average family has one or two children.

The average age of marriage is thirty-two for men and thirty for women.

The divorce rate is about 40 percent, similar to the United States and Canada.

About 61 percent of mothers work part time, so they can be home when their children are not in school.

About one-quarter of moms do not work outside their home, and 16 percent work full time.

Women are generally paid about 17 percent less than men doing the same job; this is a larger difference than in most of Europe.

As in the United States and Canada, weekends are a time for outdoor activities and sports. In the summer, walking and hiking are popular, and in the winter Swiss families enjoy skiing, snowboarding, sledding, and ice-skating. Sunday is a family day in Switzerland, and shops are closed.

Winter Vacation

All Swiss schools close for ten days or two weeks in February. This is known as the *Sportferien* (sport vacation), and many families take advantage of this time to go skiing. Although some of Switzerland's ski resorts are known for their social scene and nightlife, all of them welcome families and have special slopes and trails for beginners as well as steep trails for experts. These resorts also have ice-skating and tobogganing. At St. Moritz, families can even take a thrilling ride down the Olympic bobsled run.

City Life, Country Life

Life is different for people who live in cities and those who live in small towns and rural areas. While adults in big cities like Lausanne and Zürich can enjoy many lively neighborhoods filled with restaurants, cafés, and places to dance and listen to music, small town social life is more likely to mean sharing a meal at home with friends. Two of Switzerland's most traditional foods, fondue and raclette, seem designed for small groups of friends to share. Fondue is a pot of melted cheese that everyone dips bread into, and raclette is a cheese that is heated on a grill in the center of the table.

Swiss enjoy a warm snack of fondue outside on a snowy day. Fondue is often considered the Swiss national dish.

Since long ago, when farmers produced nearly everything their families ate, the Swiss have prized locally grown vegetables, meats, and dairy products. City dwellers who don't have backyard gardens can buy fresh-picked vegetables and farm-raised meats and eggs at farmers' markets, which are common even in large cities. The stylish lakeside resort of Vevey has one of Europe's biggest market squares, and it's filled with farmers and shoppers two mornings each week.

A shopper admires the vegetables at a market in Basel.

Good to Eat

The Swiss are very aware of healthy eating, and they avoid packaged foods from the grocery store. Whole grains and fresh vegetables were popular in Switzerland long before "health foods" caught on elsewhere. This movement began in Zürich as early as 1897, when Dr. Max Bircher-Benner opened a clinic that treated unwell people by first changing their diet. Today, Dr. Bircher-Benner is best remembered as the creator of the favorite Swiss breakfast cereal called bircher muesli, which is made from oats, fruit, and nuts. The world's first vegetarian restaurant is in Zürich, founded in 1898 by Ambrosius Hiltl and is one of the city's most popular places to eat.

Bread and cheese are staples of the Swiss diet.

Cheeses for sale in the Zürich train station. Swiss farmers produce more than 450 different kinds of cheeses.

Since cheese keeps much longer than milk, in the past it was natural for Swiss dairy farmers to turn some of their milk into cheese. In fact, the longer some cheese is kept, the better it tastes. Over time, the Swiss became known for their fine cheeses, which are used in everything from hearty soup to cheesecake. Some of the best-known Swiss cheeses include Gruyère, a hard cheese with a nutty flavor, Emmental, a mild medium-hard cheese, and raclette, a medium-firm cheese that is often used for melting.

Like everything else in Switzerland, there is no single style of Swiss cooking. Ravioli is popular in the Italian canton Ticino. In the German-speaking regions, a dumpling called spaetzle is a favorite. In the French-speaking cantons, traditional French crêpes are popular.

One dish that is typical in most areas is *rösti*, a fried potato cake that is something like American hash brown potatoes. Crisply browned and piping hot, these potato cakes can be part of a hearty mountain breakfast or can accompany dinner in a fancy Zürich restaurant. Another popular meal is the *Berner Platte*, or Bernese platter, a hearty platter piled high with roasted pork, bacon, sausages, ham, and other meats over a mound of sauerkraut.

Many Swiss pastries include fruit.

Swiss cooks, especially those from the Engadin region in the southeast, are known for their delicious cakes and pastries. Chocolate is a favorite ingredient, as are the cherries that grow around Zug, between Zürich and Lucerne. Almonds and other nuts are often ground and used to replace some of the flour in cakes and cookies.

Celebrating Together

Holidays and festivals are a good time for families and friends to get together. Because Switzerland is

Mailänderli

Mailänderli cookies are popular any time of year, but they are most common around Christmas. They are usually cut into stars, hearts, or crescent shapes, but other small cookie cutters can also be used. Have an adult help you.

Ingredients

1 cup plus 1 tablespoon butter

3¾ cups flour

1¼ cups sugar

3 eggs

Grated rind of one lemon

⅛ teaspoon salt

1 egg yolk

Small cookie cutters

Directions

Cut 1 cup butter into small pieces in a bowl and add all ingredients except the egg yolk. Mix well until the butter is blended in smoothly. Knead the mixture quickly with your hands to form a compact ball, and let dough rest in the refrigerator for at least 30 minutes. Use the remaining butter to grease a baking sheet so the cookies will not stick. After the dough has chilled, roll it out on a lightly floured surface until it is about ⅛ inch thick. Use cookie cutters to cut the dough into shapes. Place the cookie shapes on a buttered baking sheet. Beat the egg yolk and brush it carefully onto the cookies. Bake in an oven at 400°F for about 20 minutes, or until the cookies are golden. Cool the cookies on a rack, and then enjoy!

made up of people from many different backgrounds, there are few nationwide holiday customs.

Many festivals are religious in origin. Carnival, for example, is an exuberant celebration held right before Lent, the somber period leading up to Easter. Many Swiss cities hold a carnival, but the largest is in Basel, which holds its event after Lent begins. During the Carnival of Basel, fifteen to twenty thousand people put on elaborate masked costumes and parade through the streets, playing loud music and throwing confetti.

Members of bands dress as masked figures for the Basel carnival.

People of every background visit the Christmas markets that spring up in all regions in late November. These street markets are colorful "villages" of stalls shaped like little cabins. Most of the stalls sell gifts, foods, and Christmas decorations. Booths are filled with wreaths, hand-knit mittens and scarves, wooden toys, candy, and delicious cookies and cakes. Groups of musicians perform and, often, choirs of school children sing carols. In Zürich, young children dressed in green and wearing red hats sing from a platform shaped like a Christmas tree.

Shoppers visit a Christmas market in Basel.

In the Ticino canton, near Italy, nearly every town and village sets up Christmas scenes, called *presepi*, representing the birth of Jesus. The little village of Vira displays more than twenty of these scenes. Large lighted skating rinks fill city squares and chalet-shaped booths sell cookies and sweet fruit bread called *panettone*. It's easy to see why children all over Switzerland look forward to December.

During the winter months, an ice-skating rink is set up outside the Federal Palace in Bern.

Public Holidays

The only national holiday in Switzerland is National Day, on August 1. All other holidays are determined by the cantons. A few days, however, are public holidays in all twenty-six cantons. They are New Year's Day, Ascension Day—a religious holiday that usually falls in May—and Christmas. Many other holidays are observed in some or most of the cantons. On these days, schools and businesses are closed in those cantons.

Timeline

SWISS HISTORY		WORLD HISTORY	
Modern humans arrive in what is now Switzerland.	12,000 years ago		
		ca. 2500 BCE	The Egyptians build the pyramids and the Sphinx in Giza.
The Helvetians arrive in the region.	ca. 100 BCE	ca. 563 BCE	The Buddha is born in India.
The Romans take control of Helvetia.	58 BCE		
The Romans lose control of Helvetia to Germanic tribes.	400 CE	313 CE	The Roman emperor Constantine legalizes Christianity.
The monastery of St. Maurice d'Augune is founded in Valais Canton.	515		
		610	The Prophet Muhammad begins preaching a new religion called Islam.
		1054	The Eastern (Orthodox) and Western (Roman Catholic) Churches break apart.
The city of Bern is founded.	1191	1095	The Crusades begin.
		1215	King John seals the Magna Carta.
The cantons of Schwyz, Uri, and Unterwalden agree to the Oath of Rütli, creating the Swiss Confederation.	1291	1300s	The Renaissance begins in Italy.
		1347	The plague sweeps through Europe.
		1453	Ottoman Turks capture Constantinople, conquering the Byzantine Empire.
The Swiss fight the Swabian War.	1499	1492	Columbus arrives in North America.
Huldrych Zwingli leads the Protestant Reformation in Zürich.	1520s	1500s	Reformers break away from the Catholic Church, and Protestantism is born.
John Calvin settles in Switzerland and becomes a leader in the Reformation.	1533		
The Watchmakers Guild of Geneva is established.	1601		
		1776	The U.S. Declaration of Independence is signed.
The Helvetic Republic is established in an attempt to unify the cantons.	1798	1789	The French Revolution begins.

SWISS HISTORY

The Swiss Confederation is recognized as an independent country.	**1815**
A brief civil war called the Sonderbund War erupts.	**1847**
The first Swiss Federal Constitution is approved by the people; Bern is named the country's capital.	**1848**
A new constitution is approved, increasing federal influence over the cantons; purchasing the service of Swiss soldiers as mercenaries is outlawed.	**1874**
Switzerland, Germany, and Italy accomplish the massive engineering feat of the St. Gotthard Pass, the first rail pass through the Alps.	**1880**
The International Olympic Committee is founded by a Swiss man named Pierre de Coubertin.	**1894**
The Swiss National Park is established.	**1914**
The Swiss government agrees to stop accepting Jewish refugees.	**1938**
Swiss residents vote to grant women the right to vote.	**1971**
Switzerland's most recent constitution takes effect.	**2000**
Switzerland joins the United Nations.	**2002**
The right to paid maternity leave is guaranteed by federal law.	**2004**
Voters approve police and immigration cooperation with the European Union.	**2005**
Voters approve a ban on minarets.	**2009**

WORLD HISTORY

1865	The American Civil War ends.
1879	The first practical lightbulb is invented.
1914	World War I begins.
1917	The Bolshevik Revolution brings communism to Russia.
1929	A worldwide economic depression begins.
1939	World War II begins.
1945	World War II ends.
1969	Humans land on the Moon.
1975	The Vietnam War ends.
1989	The Berlin Wall is torn down as communism crumbles in Eastern Europe.
1991	The Soviet Union breaks into separate states.
2001	Terrorists attack the World Trade Center in New York City and the Pentagon near Washington, D.C.
2004	A tsunami in the Indian Ocean destroys coastlines in Africa, India, and Southeast Asia.
2008	The United States elects its first African American president.

Fast Facts

Official name: Swiss Confederation

Capital: Bern

Official languages: German, French, Italian, Rumantsch

Official religion: None

Bern

National flag

National anthem:	"Schweizerpsalm" ("Swiss Psalm")
Type of government:	Confederation
Head of state:	Federal Council
Head of government:	Federal Council
Area of country:	15,940 square miles (41,285 sq km)
Latitude and longitude of geographic center:	47°00' N, 8°00' E
Bordering countries:	Germany to the north, France to the west, Italy to the south, Austria and Liechtenstein to the east
Highest elevation:	Dufourspitze, 15,203 feet (4,634 m) above sea level
Lowest elevation:	Lake Maggiore, 640 feet (195 m) above sea level
Longest river:	Rhine, 233 miles (375 km) within Switzerland
Longest lake:	Lake Geneva, 45 miles (73 km)
Largest glacier:	Aletsch Glacier, 66 square miles (171 sq km)
Average daily high temperature:	In Zürich, 38°F (3°C) in January, 75°F (24°C) in July
Average daily low temperature:	In Zürich, 28°F (–2°C) in January, 57°F (14°C) in July

Matterhorn

Abbey of St. Gall

Currency

National population (2014 est.):	8,237,700	
Population of major cities (2014 est.):	Zürich	391,400
	Geneva	194,600
	Basel	168,600
	Lausanne	133,900
	Bern	130,000

Landmarks:

▶ *Abbey of St. Gall*, St. Gallen

▶ *Hölloch Cave*, Schwyz canton

▶ *Lion Monument*, Lucerne

▶ *Matterhorn*, Valais canton

▶ *Rütli meadow*, Uri canton

Economy: Switzerland's dominant industry is services, most importantly international banking and tourism. Switzerland is also well known for its very high-quality precision instruments such as watches. Other major manufactured products include pharmaceuticals and food products such as chocolate. Major agricultural products include sugar beets, wheat, barley, and potatoes. Many dairy cattle are also raised in Switzerland. Much of the milk is turned into fine cheeses.

Currency: Swiss franc. In 2016, 1 Swiss franc was worth US$1.03, and US$1.00 equaled 0.97 francs.

System of weights and measures: Metric system

Literacy rate (2015): 99%

Schoolchildren

Roger Federer

Languages spoken in Switzerland:

English: *Hi*
German: *Gruezi*
French: *Salut*
Italian: *Ciao*
Rumantsch: *Tgau*

English: *Good-bye*
German: *Auf Wiedersehen*
French: *Au revoir*
Italian: *Arrivederci*
Rumantsch: *Sin seveser*

Prominent Swiss:

Le Corbusier (1887–1965)
Architect

Ruth Dreifuss (1940–)
First female president of the Swiss Confederation

Guillaume-Henri Dufour (1787–1875)
Army general who cofounded the Red Cross

Jean-Henri Dunant (1828–1910)
Humanitarian who cofounded the Red Cross

Roger Federer (1981–)
Tennis player

Paul Klee (1879–1940)
Artist

Daniel Peter (1836–1919)
Chocolatier

Johanna Spyri (1827–1901)
Novelist

To Find Out More

Books

- ▶ Peppas, Lynn. *The Alps*. St. Catherines, Ontario, Canada: Crabtree Publishing, 2011.

- ▶ Rappaport, Doreen. *Beyond Courage: The Untold Story of Jewish Resistance During the Holocaust*. Somerville, MA: Candlewick Press, 2112.

- ▶ Spyri, Johanna. *Heidi*. London: Puffin Books, 2014.

Music

- ▶ *Air Mail Music: Traditional Instruments of Switzerland*. Boulogne, France: Playasound, 2000.

- ▶ *Voyager: Edelweiss*. Portland, OR: Columbia River Entertainment Group, 2001.

▶ Visit this Scholastic Web site for more information on Switzerland:
www.factsfornow.scholastic.com
Enter the keyword Switzerland

Index

Page numbers in *italics*
indicate illustrations.

national holiday, 127
national park, 28, 37, *37*
Nazi Party, 57–58, 59, 60, 61, *61*, 107
Neanderthals, 39
Nestlé chocolates, 82
Neuchâtel canton, 51, 56, 63, 72
neutrality, 56, 62–63, 115
New Year's Day, 127
Nicholas of Flüe, 45
Nobel Peace Prize, 54

O
Oath of Rütli, 42, *42*, 44
Olympic Games, 24, 103, 113, 114–115, *115*, 118

P
panettone (fruit bread), 127
people. *See also* education; employment.
    Alamannen, 41
    children, 13, 90–91, 109, 117, 118
    clothing, *100, 110*
    diversity of, 24
    divorce, 118
    early settlers, 38, 39, 95
    families, 100, 101, *116*, 117, 118, *118*, 123
    Franks, 41
    funerals, 101
    Germanic tribes, 41
    health care, 54, *54*
    Helvetians, 40
    immigrants, 65, *65*, 72, 86
    Jews, 59, 60, *60*, 61, 68
    marriage, 100, *101*, 118
    Neanderthals, 39
    permanent foreign residents, 24, 65
    population, 15, 24, 71, 85–87, 86
    refugees, 59, 60, *60*
    Romans, 40–41, *41*

sovereignty of, 67
urban areas, 119
Verdingkinder ("contract children"), 13
voting rights, 72
women, 63–64, *64*, 118
permanent foreign residents, 24, 65
Peter, Daniel, 82, 133
petitions, 72, *72*
pharmaceutical industry, 81, *81*
pine martens, 34, *34*
plant life
    avalanches and, 32
    chestnuts, 33, *33*
    climate and, 31
    edelweiss, 32, *32*
    elevation and, 31–32
    southern regions, 31, 33
    Swiss National Park, 37
    trees, 31, 100
Poland, 58
population, 15, 24, 71, 85–87, 86
poya painting, 103–104
presepi (Christmas scenes), 127
presidents, 69
Pro Natura organization, 28
Protestantism, 47–49, 97–98, 100

Q
queen cows, 79

R
raclette cheese, 119, 122
railroads, 8, 18, 19, 20–22, *21*, 55
recipe, 124, *124*
Red Cross, 52, 54, *54*, 133
referendums, 72
refugees, 59, 60, *60*
religion. *See also* Roman Catholic Church.
    art and, 49
    baptisms, 100
    cantons and, 98

early settlers and, 95
Federation of Swiss Protestant Churches, 97–98
government and, 97–98, 99
holidays, 100, 125–127
Huldrych Zwingli and, *47*, 48
Islam, 99, *99*
Jesuits, 53
John Calvin and, 48, *48*
Judaism, 59, 60
mosques, 99, *99*
mythology, 95–96
national flag and, 68
observation of, 100
Protestantism, 47–49, 97–98, 100
Swiss Diet and, *53*
Swiss Guards, 45, *45*
Swiss Reformed Church, 98, *98*
Rhine River, 16, 26
Rhône River, 26
roadways, 19, *19*, 20, 74
Roberts of Kandahar Challenge Cup, 113
Roman Catholic Church. *See also* religion.
    Abbey of St. Gall, 97, *97*
    government and, 98
    Jesuits, 53
    Lausanne Cathedral, *94*
    marriage and, *101*
    Middle Ages, 47
    observation of, 100
    Protestant Reformation and, 47–49, 52, *53*
    St. Gallen Cathedral, 97, *97*
    St. Maurice d'Augune monastery, 96
    Swiss Guards, 45, *45*
    Vatican City, 45
Roman Empire, 40–41, *41*
Röstigraben, 88

Meet the Author

LURA ROGERS SEAVEY WAS ELEVEN YEARS old when she first traveled to Switzerland. On that trip, she visited Lucerne and the glacial tunnels at Mount Titlis. Two years later, she returned to explore Switzerland's lakes by boat and to hike in the Alps.

For Seavey, the most enjoyable part of writing and researching this book was visiting Swiss towns and villages, where she talked to local people and learned more about their life and customs. On her most recent travels to Geneva, she took her eleven-year-old daughter, Mary, on her own first trip to Switzerland.

Seavey studied at Skidmore College in New York and Harvard University in Massachusetts, where she received a Bachelor of Arts degree. She has written several other books in the Enchantment of the World series, including *Spain* and *Dominican Republic*. She is also the author of *More Than Petticoats: Remarkable Massachusetts Women*, a collection of short biographies.

Photo Credits